Souls of Someone

PRAISE FOR SOULS OF SOMEONE

Souls of Someone is a remarkable, moving visual diary, capturing not just a festival but also a layered world of women, with all their strengths, vulnerabilities, faith and agency. There is love, laughter, sorrow and a whole spectrum of emotions, related by a witness and a friend, with respect, affection and a willingness to learn and unlearn. A beautiful tribute, this book is also an expression of hope for a better, more accepting world. I learned a great deal from it.

—Manu S. Pillai

Souls of Someone

MYTH, MAGIC *and* MOURNING *in* KOOVAGAM

SHINO CHERIAN

PHOTOGRAPHS BY

Shino Cherian
Ram Manu Prasad
Praveen Kumar Raja

HarperCollins *Publishers* India

First published in India by HarperCollins Publishers 2026
HarperCollins *Publishers* India, Cyber City,
Building 10-A, Gurugram, Haryana – 122002, India
www.harpercollins.co.in

2 4 6 8 10 9 7 5 3 1

P-ISBN: 9789369891269
E-ISBN: 9789369891023

Typeset in 10.5/14 Adobe Caslon Pro
by HarperCollins *Publishers* India Pvt. Ltd

Printed in India by Multivista Global Pvt. Ltd.

FSC www.fsc.org
MIX
Paper | Supporting responsible forestry
FSC® C199630

HarperCollins Publishers, Macken House, 39/40 Mayor Street Upper, Dublin 1, D01 C9W8, Ireland

Some sort of pressure must exist; the artist exists because the world is not perfect. Art would be useless if the world were perfect, as man wouldn't look for harmony but would simply live in it. Art is born out of an ill-designed world.

—ANDREI TARKOVSKY

Agara mudhala ezhuthellam aadhi bhagawan mudhatre ulagu

'A' is the beginning of all letters, the foundational letter;
God is the foundational and foremost entity of the universe.

—TIRUKKUṞAḶ, THIRUVALLUVAR

CONTENTS

FOREWORD

WHEN IT RAINS, IT POURS; AND THEN THE SUN SHINES AGAIN

Claude Monet, the French Impressionist, once told his friend Georges Clemenceau that even as his beloved wife Camille lay dying, he caught himself focusing on her temples, automatically analyzing the succession of appropriately graded colors that death was imposing on her motionless face. 'There were blue, yellow, grey tones—tones I cannot describe,' Monet said. This was the point he had reached as an artist; breaking the conventions of his time, attracted to scenes of dissolution, and tormented by tireless obsessions with colour. The author of this book, Shino Cherian, shares Monet's instinctive picture-making tendency. Upon seeing photos of trans women in Koovagam for the first time on his friend Manu's phone, this is what he notices: 'My mind's eye brimmed with a variety of images—gold against brown skin, vermillion-streaked hair catching the light, multicoloured garlands bright against the ancient grey stones of the temple.' Colours and light seem to fascinate Shino equally in his search for truth and his scouring for the soul and magic of Koovagam.

As in Monet's anecdote, death and grief occupy a major part of this book as well. The Koovagam festival is an annual eighteen-day gathering of trans women during the month of Chithirai in the Tamil calendar. Shino and Manu, along with the kind individuals and families they meet in Koovagam, unravel the different rituals and mythologies behind the festival. The most prevalent history is that trans women come together in the form of Mohini, acting as symbolic brides to the deity Iravan/Aravan/Koothandavar, who was sacrificed to win the eighteen-day Kurukshetra war. Festivals such as Koovagam or Oor Thiruvizhas play a vital role in the lives of trans women who have been abandoned and ostracized by both family and society. These Thiruvizhas become sites of both celebration and revolution for us, where the act of being seen is the greatest victory of all. My daughter, Sri Akshaya, writes about this too, in her recently published autobiography, *Kovilpatti to Chennai Vazhi(li)thadangal.*

As Shino prepares to travel to Koovagam and witness the festival on his own, he carries with him the baggage that many outsiders do. He enters Koovagam with his camera, at first, like a shield against the unknown. But eventually, as he immerses himself in the the event and its layered histories, he opens his heart to unlearn and relearn. He is compelled to write this book because my community of sisters, mothers and daughters demanded that he *see* them.

The brilliance of this work lies in Shino's willingness to 'unbecome' the person he thought he was. He admits to his early hesitations, the knot in his chest and the queasiness of overthinking. He documents the moment he realizes that pointing a camera at a trans woman bathing in a pond (which alludes to Sir John Everett Millais's *Ophelia* except the Ophelia here is not drowning, but surfacing) made him feel like a voyeur. It is this awareness and vulnerability that make the work so riveting; it helps the reader understand that this is indeed an 'ill-designed world', and art and resistance ache to be born out of it.

What is particularly striking to me is the book's ability to let the reader ponder grief. There are stunning images of a bevy of trans women, who, adorned on the penultimate day of the festival in bright saris, bangles and thalis, appear as widows of Aravan on the last day as he is sacrificed; their hair disheveled, their saris white, deep in mourning. Grief has always been difficult for me to process; no words can rightly articulate how I feel about it. However, I see my feelings reflected closely in an image in the book, where a trans woman walks alone in a wide field. Perhaps I have developed a penchant for this image because of the unearthly sense it evokes. The trans women appear more determined than ever in their white saris. Perhaps grief (a misunderstood emotion?) is much like that. We do not grieve to end grief; rather, we grieve because it shows our capacity to care. As a friend once said, it shows our refusal to close ourselves off from the power of love, even if it was that same power that exposed us to the weight of loss.

Moving through this grief is not just about the martyrdom of Aravan; it is symbolic of the grief we face when our birth families beg us to leave and the grief of this ill-designed society. Even then, we have managed to find families and infinite love within our community—as readers will see in this book. It is also important to mention the centrality of love and care in the process of grief, as both are a vital antidote to oppression, as rightly pointed out by scholars such as bell hooks, Ursula K. Le Guin, and Babasaheb Ambedkar.

In this book, we see the lives of trans women who have faced continuous rejection by the society, yet are always ready and resilient to face the world and flourish. There is a grain of hope we all hold on to, beautifully expressed by Shino in the phrase 'when it rains, it pours' (providentially, as Rajendran anna predicts in the book, on the night of the marriage of the many trans women to the deity Aravan, the sky pours its heart out). To complete the idiom, 'the sun will always shine again'. Just as the grief of the trans women passes, a new beginning awaits every year at Koovagam. For all those who feel lost, the 'Amsterdam of Tamil Nadu' offers comfort and a sense of belonging, whether you are a curious traveler or a restless soul searching to belong.

The Koovagam festival has gained significant attention in the last few years, and this book is a pioneering work in documenting and archiving the cultural richness of Tamil Nadu, in which trans women play a vital part. One might easily interpret the 'souls' as the subjects of the photos, but interestingly, towards the end of the book, the writer grounds the title in his own experience of having transformed into his actual self—the 'very soul of someone', no longer an outsider; his camera no longer a shield, but a *witness.*

Shino has captured the magic, the truth, and the souls of Koovagam who refuse to be dissolved. I invite the readers to bear witness to these stories, the photos and the folklore; for in the end, as Shino discovers, we are all 'looking to be complete by the folklore of the discreet.'

Grace Banu
February 2026

PROLOGUE

'Where am I when I am not in reality or imagination?'

—DOMENICO (ERLAND JOSEPHSON), IN ANDREI TARKOVSKY'S *Nostalghia* (1983)

In 2018, Ram Manu Prasad, a friend from NEO Film School, and I were working on a photoshoot for a client in Chennai. Complete opposites, we had not got to know each other until the final semester while we were studying. He was born and raised in Marayoor, a small village in southwestern Kerala known for its sandalwood forests, ancient dolmens and rock paintings from the Stone Age. I was raised in Chennai, a city boy who'd been through different schools and mingled with people of different backgrounds and cultures. Our worlds collided only in the darkroom, where light and shadow revealed a shared desire to capture the 'truth'. We'd lost touch after the course and only met again in Marayoor while I was filming a documentary there.

Now, we were back in Chennai, and the city loaned a different flavour to our interactions. Though Manu and I had both transitioned from being film school students to working professionals, the differences between us remained clear and in many ways the same—his calm, grounded presence shaped by Marayoor was in stark contrast to my restlessness honed by years of navigating a hectic urban existence.

Around this time, I felt a growing hollowness inside me, after years of freelance gigs consisting of weddings, corporate shoots and photographing newborns. While the work was fun to an extent, I'd become a stranger to my own life, documenting joy for others while my creativity, my own joy, starved. But to survive, what other choice did one have?

I had not thought about doing a full-time job and 'settling' down.

I am not sure my parents had either, although my amma is the ambitious one in the family. They later decided that I should choose what to do with my career, which is how I ended up following my passion of photography and filmmaking.

After wrapping the shoot in Chennai, Manu and I packed our gear and boarded the bus to our home in Ashok Nagar. It was a highly congested area where the noise from vehicles was cacophonous in the evening as the traffic was at its peak. But really, people crowded the streets at all times here. Suddenly pulling out his phone, Manu showed me some Instagram images tagged #HumansOfKoovagam—radiant photos of transgender people in paddy fields, their saris blazing like the countless shades of a glorious sunset.

'Interesting images. Where did you find these?' I asked.

'I was just scrolling through Instagram when these images popped up. These photos were taken at the Koovagam Koothandavar Thiruvizha or the Koovagam festival, where people celebrate the legend of the wedding of Aravan, Arjun's son, and Mohini, Krishna's only female avatar and transgender identity,' said Manu.

Manu showed me a few more pictures of the transgender people at the event, each one more fascinating and intriguing than the one before it.

The images burned themselves into my mind—vibrant attires against green fields, proud faces that refused to be dissolved into oblivion. This wasn't merely photography; this was testimony, resistance, celebration; all rolled into one. My fingers itched for my camera.

'It would be fun to visit and document this festival,' said Manu.

Manu, who grew up in Marayoor, was always interested in agronomy, the customs and chronicles of a place, and the people and its surroundings. I was tired, worn out and sleepy after a long day at work—but the moment I heard those words, I perked up and turned to look at him.

'Shall we?'

'What?' he asked, confused.

'Shall we go to this festival and document it?'

Just then, our bus stop was called. We hurried down the steps as some schoolboys and their parents got off as well. Our street was accessible only by foot, so we'd usually get off on the main road and walk through many narrow lanes to reach home.

'Let's do it,' replied Manu softly, as we turned into a lane.

That simple phrase set my heart racing. For the first time in months, I felt awake, alive. This wasn't just another job—it was a chance to reclaim a purpose, why I'd picked up a camera in the first place.

As we were to learn later: every year between April and May, thousands of transgender individuals converge at Koothandavar Temple in Viluppuram for the eighteen-day Koovagam festival. For the first sixteen days, the now-famous Miss Koovagam beauty pageant and other cultural performances and programmes are organized. On the seventeenth day, the attendees dress up in their finest as symbolic brides of the deity Aravan, with colourful bangles and resplendent jewellery, and celebrate their marriage to the deity. They also tie thalis (mangalsutras) around their necks and apply kumkum on their foreheads. The final day of the festival is marked for mourning the death of their divine husband, in honour of the legend described in the Mahabharata.

When I saw the photos from the festival on Manu's phone, my mind's eye brimmed with a variety of images—gold against brown skin, vermillion-streaked hair catching the light, multicoloured garlands bright against the ancient grey stones of the temple.

As we continued to walk towards our house and look at the photos in between, we realized that the festival was about to end in another couple of days. 'It's almost over. Let's go next year,' I said hesitantly.

'No, wait' said Manu. 'The last two days of the festival are when the main events are organized,' he murmured. His quiet voice cut through my doubts as he checked Google Maps on his phone. 'Viluppuram is only 180 kilometres away. We could be there in four hours by train from Chennai.'

In that moment, the fog of routine clouding my head cleared. Here was a story pulsing with life, one that the rigmarole of commercial photography could never contain. 'Let's do it,' I said. 'Let's leave tomorrow morning.'

'Are you sure?' asked Manu.

'Yes. Yes, I'm absolutely sure.'

In that moment, I recalled how important it is to entertain the idea that sticks in your mind; to feed it well, make it part of you, for this sudden burst of inspiration can, in turn, inscribe your name in the hearts of people. Partly out of an unheeded boredom within him and partly out of his own curiosity about the Koovagam festival, Manu nodded.

Our decision to visit the festival and document the transgender community had come together in the last ten minutes of our walk back home.

Before reaching home, we stopped at a Café Coffee Day outlet. Manu looked a bit disconcerted.

'Is everything fine? Are you okay?' I asked.

'Yes, I am—thank you.'

We sat in silence for a little while. I knew from experience that Manu was quite reticent and kept his feelings to himself usually. I could also sense that his responsibilities weighed heavily on him—the family land, his brother's education, the expectations that came with being the eldest child. This impulsive trip was everything his careful life wasn't. And yet, there seemed to be a light in his eyes I hadn't seen in a while.

One morning, Manu had been looking at my pictures and he said to me, 'You're good at what you do, Shino. You capture a frame at the right time.'

When I asked how he got into photography, Manu had only smiled and replied, 'This profession is what keeps me active and alive.'

Every photographer in the world can viscerally understand this sentiment. There's magic in meeting new people, experiencing diverse cultures, new flavours, traditions and ways of life.

While we were still sipping our coffees, my phone rang. It was Shalini Somanath, a writer and a theatre artist from Gujarat.

I told her about the plan to go to Koovagam. As soon she heard it, she got very excited and began explaining the intricacies of the festival to me. She has always encouraged me to take initiative, and this time was no exception.

'Everything I've heard about the Koovagam festival makes it sound like it's truly one of its kind. It's the only transgender festival of its scale in India. Plus, you'll also meet a lot of fellow photographers and journalists from across the subcontinent, so you won't be alone. You should go if you can!'

'I'm thrilled about going to the festival—but also a little scared,' I replied.

'There is *always* a first time for everything, Shino. Remember, life isn't just about taking in oxygen and giving out carbon dioxide. You *must* put yourself out there and experience it.'

Those were exactly the words I needed to hear as both conviction and fortitude suddenly swept through me. I felt a childlike happiness, and the thought of a new beginning, a new adventure with my camera made my heart beat faster with excitement.

I thanked Shalini for speaking with me and for motivating me at exactly the right time. She took an audible breath, laughed and said, 'I am merely spreading the energy of love all around me; it is more powerful than the forces of darkness; the god within me greets the god who lives in all the inhabitants of this place.'

And that is when it hit me—aren't we all seekers in some way, navigating this vast universe? I have always felt joyful about taking on new adventures. I have always believed that if you embrace spontaneity, you begin to see how everything around you—nature, people and passing moments—shape and transform your thoughts and teach you lessons in ways you could never have imagined.

Those conversations with Manu and Shalini became the spark I needed, inspiring me to take that first step on a path of new learning. And so, I was led to Koovagam.

When I returned home after the festival, I knew that everything I had seen in a scant few days had changed me. The kindness of strangers, the challenges I faced, the rich culture and belief systems I came across and the adventures I stumbled into … But most significantly, it was the transgender individuals I had met—their bold, refreshing perspectives on life, their courage and their profound and unflinching understanding of themselves had left the most lasting impact on me. Paulo Coelho expressed this best in *The Alchemist*, 'Tell your heart that the fear of suffering is worse than the suffering itself. And that no heart has ever suffered when it goes in search of its dreams, because every second of the search is a second's encounter with god and eternity.' I lived the truth in this quote during my time at Koovagam. And all of it felt too powerful to keep to just myself.

As the days passed after my return, my need to preserve this experience, to not let it fade away into nostalgia and memory grew stronger with each passing day. So, I decided to write a book—not just to document what I had seen, but to discover something new within myself.

PART 1

THE DILEMMA

29 APRIL

Once Manu and I had finished our coffees and were walking back home, I pulled up some articles about Koovagam posted by travellers and journalists on the internet. Not many details had been shared about the place or its people but nearly everyone who had visited described it as an awe-inspiring experience.

After a long day of work, a strange, delicious calm settles on you when you return to a room of your own. That night, after reading a bit online, I lay down and tried to close my eyes. *Sleep. Sleep. Sleep.* I kept telling myself. But my thoughts were already elsewhere and my mind had kicked into overdrive. *How will we reach the Koovagam festival safely? What else will we need to carry other than our camera equipment? What will we do there? Should we be going there this year or the next?*

I got out of bed, took my laptop from my bag and started looking for information about the Koovagam festival again.

As I scrolled through articles, I came across some interesting facts about this small town in the Viluppuram district of Tamil Nadu. Koovagam appears insignificant on the map, but once a year, it transforms into the biggest gathering of transgender people from across India. I paused for a fraction of a second and a sudden memory flashed through my mind in that moment.

It was 2016, and I was on a train to Varanasi. I was working as an assistant director for a music video then, carrying my first serious camera, a Canon 660D with a kit lens. I was just beginning to explore photography, deeply inspired by Steve McCurry's street photography—especially his ability to capture raw humanity, the soul of everyday life. In that crowded compartment, a trans woman approached me.

She asked me to give her some money, but I had very little to spare, unfortunately, and politely told her so. She was not quite pleased with my response. The situation quickly escalated into an uncomfortable violation with forceful touching and aggressive cajoling. Even though there were other passengers nearby, I was the chosen target, seemingly. After arguing for an interminable hour, I surrendered the little money I had on me at that time.

I was left quite shaken by this event and thought about it for many days. In India, it seems that such encounters are quite common. Due to a lack of economic opportunities—often perpetuated by social biases—the transgender community depends on benefactions. Most of us might have encountered transgender people during our travels, appealing to our charitable moods to offer them some money and take their blessings in turn. While most trans people accept whatever amount is offered, give their blessings and move along, there are others who can sometimes resort to harassment to extract as much money as they can. Unfortunately, the experience had such a strong impact on me, that for many years, I used to become paranoid every time I was in the vicinity of trans people, while waiting at a red light on the road or while travelling in trains, fearing that the unpleasant incident might be repeated. Naturally, even as I was charged up to visit Koovagam, a part of me was alert and perhaps a bit afraid, too. We all carry wounds, some inflicted unknowingly, but real growth comes from confronting them. As I was to learn later, though, the festival would help me in more ways than I can list.

As I dug deeper into my research that night, I found out that celebrations in Koovagam generally reach their crescendo on Chitra Pournami, the full moon day of the Chaitra month of the Hindu calendar, considered an extremely auspicious time of spiritual power. Of the many unique, and perhaps even strange festivals observed in India, the Koothandavar festival stands apart because of the ancient rituals it champions and the marginalized community at its heart—making it one of the most unconventional celebrations on earth.

I picked up the diary lying on the table and pulled out a pen from the desk. The curtains swayed in the breeze coming in from outside.

Clouds drifted across the sky, some clustered together, others floating apart. I felt the urge to write down my thoughts, something I've done regularly since I was in school.

Most of these individuals, those we label as transgender, eunuch, hijra, aravani, etc., have been pushed to the margins. They are forced to be the left-out, underprivileged victims of prejudice. Some have carved out social positions against all odds as teachers, labourers, entrepreneurs, but many still struggle, working as sex workers, begging on the streets or living alone. Most of them are compelled to live a lonely life and along with all the injustice that they have to endure, they must also confront another sadness: the inability to marry and establish a family of their own. The Koovagam festival allows them this chance—a time when they can finally be themselves, celebrated for who they are rather than ostracized. I'm in equal part thrilled and terrified at the opportunity to witness this precious moment, to document how they embrace this hard-won joy. I hope my camera can do justice to their emotions.

I closed the diary, feeling that my thoughts had leaped out of the page and surrounded me in the room. A few drops of rain fell on the windowpane and seconds later the skies opened up. Heavy raindrops fell onto the muddy ground, dappling the leaves of the plant near the window.

I turned to my laptop to check for accommodation near Viluppuram. However, there were hardly any vacant hotel rooms and the one that was available was more than 27 kilometres away from Koovagam. My enthusiasm was dampened, just like the drenched leaves outside. Where were we going to stay? Would outsiders be welcomed by the transgender community and the villagers? Especially photographers like us? Also, we would have our camera gear on us, so wandering around or sleeping just about anywhere was not at all an option. I felt a knot tighten in my chest as these thoughts piled up. I was starting to feel queasy, overthinking every detail.

So, I shut down my laptop and moved to the balcony to get some fresh air. The city lights were still on, and I could hear the hum of traffic, the occasional honk, and dogs barking somewhere nearby. It is true that a city like Chennai never sleeps. Time passed, and my questions and doubts began to lose their hold on me.

30 APRIL

I woke up around 9 a.m., I checked my email, packed my clothes, camera and lens, freshened up, took my morning medicines and turned on my phone to check whether it had been charged overnight. I then sat down with my diary and made a checklist for the journey to Koovagam: food, water, camera, money, clothes, handbooks for scribbling notes, pen, reading glasses, Manu. Oh! But where was Manu?

I went to the other room to check on him. I found him already awake, dressed and quietly packing up his gear. We didn't talk much—both of us were lost in our own thoughts, the weight of what lay ahead making the silence feel natural, even necessary.

We left for the closest railway station, pausing for breakfast at Lakshmi Nivas near the Saidapet Karaneeswarar temple. *I've planned everything*, I reassured myself for the hundredth time as we sat down to order. The tiny Tamil restaurant served phenomenal south Indian food—the kind that we hoped would inspire and nourish us for the journey ahead.

As we waited for our order to arrive, I pulled out my phone and texted Shalini: 'We're on our way. Thank you for the push.'

Then I continued to read some stories about the festival. I learned that during the first six days Koothandavar's head is paraded through the streets of Koovagam with music and fireworks accompanying the procession. Each household offers a puja to the head, with transgender women performing the aarti. Coconuts are offered and other rituals are observed by men at the temple. Traditionally, goats and chickens are also sacrificed. When I mentioned the last detail to Manu, he was not too pleased.

'I think I'd like to talk to the festival organizers and get them to stop killing animals. Anyway. Tell me, who is Koothandavar?' asked Manu.

'He is the deity worshiped by the transgender people at the temple. He is known as Aravan in the Mahabharata' I replied.

'So, are these stories linked to the Mahabharata?'

'Yes,' I said. 'There are a few stories about how Aravan came to be known as Koothandavar. Listen to this: After the war of Kurukshetra, when the Pandavas were proudly celebrating their victory over the Kauravas, Krishna turned to Aravan and asked, "Who really won this war?" Aravan answered, "Lord, your mighty discus cut down the enemy, and your conch gathered their blood."

'This angered Bhima because the victory of the Pandavas hinges on his crucial role in the battle. Just as Bhima was about to attack Aravan for his alleged insolence, Krishna commanded that Aravan's head be severed and thrown into the Caraparika river. There, Aravan transformed into a baby. Later, the king of Chandragiri, a city by the river, found the child. When the king picked him up, the baby cried, "Kuva Kuva!" So, the king named the place where he was found Koovagam.'

'I see, so that's how the name of the place came to be?' asked Manu.

'That's one theory, but of course, there are other stories as well. This version sounds a bit incomplete, don't you think?'

'Yes, I want to know more about all this, there seem to be some gaps in this story' Manu said eyeing his thayir vadai hungrily.

Even though I had read various accounts of the legend, I was also quite confused by so many strands coming together at Koovagam. I have to get to the bottom of this, I thought to myself, and I said the same to Manu.

'There's a lot that is still quite confusing, I hope we will learn all about it in time. It seems that the king adopted the boy, naming him Carapala. When he grew up, the boy fought and killed the demon Kuttacuran, who had injured his adoptive father in battle. Draupadi, worshipped as the mother goddess in this tale, blessed

Carapala, renaming him Kuttantavar and granting him a temple in Koovagam. Later, Krishna revealed that Aravan was always destined to slay the demon and hence he arranged for his body to be thrown into the river, to be discovered by the king ...'

The accounts of the Kurukshetra war and the killing of the demon Kuttacuran, however, seemed to suggest that there was a missing link somewhere. We would, of course, piece together the fragments in time ...

I turned to Manu and assured him that there were many such stories waiting to unfold.

'So, what's next?'

'Well, a four-and-a-half-hour journey by train starting from the Saidapet Railway Station to the Egmore Station and then on to Viluppuram. We should reach Viluppuram by 4.30 p.m.'

As we paid the bill, it struck me that our journeys shape us—sometimes, we emerge wiser, sometimes, we learn to cope after a period of strife and struggle. Wandering helps us rediscover ourselves and dismantles the protections we put up around our innermost selves.

Steve Jobs visited India before he established Apple. He went by a local train and bus to a village near Nainital, near the foothills of the Himalayas—the abode of Neem Karoli Baba. Jobs rented a room with a mattress on the floor from a family who looked after him. A previous traveller had left a copy of *Autobiography of a Yogi* in the room. Jobs read it a several times during his stay, and he walked around from village to village, a lone wanderer.

His spiritual journey to discover himself and his education in Buddhism began from here.

When I was on my way to Koovagam, I felt like I was in a similar situation. I was trying to figure out myself and my place in this world. As a middle-class Indian youth, I had chosen an unconventional path for myself as a photographer and filmmaker. I felt as if I was being led to Koovagam by a powerful force, that I would, after all, find myself there, too, doing what I loved the most, exercising my skills as an image maker.

We reached Egmore just in time. As the train to Viluppuram whistled and approached the platform, a huge crowd gathered, and as the engine slowed down, people started pushing each other to climb aboard.

'Don't worry, this is a daily event here,' said a man wearing formals and neatly polished shoes. 'You'll find your way in!'

Manu and I made sure that we held on to our equipment tightly. As soon as the train stopped, the man who had just spoken to us hopped in and sprinted to an empty seat. In a matter of seconds, we had also boarded the train. The crowd on the platform disappeared as quickly as it had appeared.

ARRIVING IN KOOVAGAM

30 APRIL

Train journeys aren't always fun, and they're even less so when you're travelling in an unreserved compartment packed to capacity on a hot Indian summer day. A couple of hours after we boarded, Manu and I managed to find a seat. We stowed our bags beneath the seat and started surfing the internet for information about the Koovagam festival.

We realized that we would be arriving at the festival on the evening of the sixteenth day. All sources confirmed that that was when the festival peaked.

The aravanis, which is the Tamil word to usually describe transgender women, arrive in Koovagam in ever-growing numbers from the fourteenth to the sixteenth day. Preceding their symbolic wedding to Aravan on the penultimate day, they dance with the flower crown of the deity, which is believed to possess his power. This is a traditional ceremony which the aravanis celebrate by singing their favourite songs.

After the ceremony of adorning the idol is complete and the ritual dance is over, on the day of the wedding, the thali ceremony begins. The thali, a traditional mark of a married woman in Tamil Nadu, is a pendant, usually made of gold or other precious metals, that is tied around the neck. In Koovagam, this takes the form of a thread with a piece of turmeric as the pendant. The priests, representing Aravan, tie the thalis around the necks of all those who wish to marry the deity in the inner sanctum of the temple—including men, in some cases, who have taken certain vows.

The night of the wedding, aravanis can have sex, which is viewed as an act of consummating the wedding. These are nights of uninhibited celebration and the expression of their love for their deity.

As Manu and I shared our notes, to our very great surprise, an old man wearing a red shawl and loose dhoti sitting next to me said in English, 'Those who marry Aravan are not described as having sex in any traditional accounts. While the aravanis wear women's clothes and jewellery, the men who marry Aravan, in fulfilment of vows made for granting their wishes, wear male clothes throughout the ritual.'

'Oh. Avalo *iruka*! There's so much more to learn!' I replied.
He continued, '*Innum iruku*, indeed. Early in the morning of the sixteenth day, it is said that Aravan's soul is transferred back to his repainted head, and the ritual of opening the god's eyes is performed by painting the pupils on the head and putting it on the katayam.'

'What is the katayam?' asked Manu.

'Aravan's head is paraded around the village on a portable platform called a katayam. This is accompanied by two platform chariots, one holding Aravan's chest plate and epaulets, without which the festival is considered incomplete, and the other carrying his flower crown.

'The marriages of the aravanis end with the sacrificial offering of roosters on the final day. Aravan's head is mounted on the post, and his epaulets and chest plate are fixed to his straw body, which is then garlanded. The figure is paraded through the village, and the ritual re-enactment of his death on the eighth day of the Mahabharata war takes place. At noon, his chariot turns north to face a predesignated area, meant to stand for Kurukshetra, symbolizing his arrival onto the battlefield to die at the hands of Alambusha.'

'Are you, by any chance, a priest at the temple, sir?' asked Manu.

The old man laughed and replied, 'No, I am just a curious traveller who has come to explore the customs and history of Koovagam, just like you, I suppose. This is my third visit to the festival, and each time, I learn and experience something new. Shall I continue the story, or are you bored?'

We nodded eagerly and so the old man continued weaving the tale for his rapt audience. 'After the parade, the vivid garlands are removed from the idol, indicating the stripping away of his flesh and his defeat on the eighth day of the Kurukshetra war. The chariot with the idol then turns towards the location prepared for the mourning rituals, the weeping grounds. The widowed aravanis, with their hair dishevelled and bangles broken, lament the death of their husband as kalappali is performed.'

'What is kalappali?' asked Manu.

'It's a ritual performed before going into battle to ensure victory. One by one, the garlands from Aravan's chariot are thrown to the devotees, signifying his gradual loss of vitality. At the weeping ground, the aravanis mourn Aravan's death by breaking their bangles, beating their breasts and discarding their bridal finery, much like in the legend of Mohini and Krishna. They cut their thalis, which are flung at a post erected for the ceremony. Then they take a bath in a nearby pond and put on white sarees as a mark of their widowhood. In the mid-afternoon, Aravan is stripped to his skeletal straw body. Most aravanis leave by then, and men wedded to Aravan also break their thalis and bangles and perform all the rites of widowhood in front of an image of Aravan. Meanwhile, a storyteller, one who is especially skilled at reciting the Mahabharata, tells the story of the culmination of the war, symbolic of Aravan fulfilling his wish of seeing the war.'

'For how many days do the aravanis remain widows?' asked Manu.

'The aravanis wear white for a month before re-adorning themselves with bangles and coloured saris,' said the old man. After a brief pause, he continued, 'At the weeping grounds, a symbolic sacrifice of cooked "blood rice" is distributed in honour of the deceased Aravan. This rice is believed to make childless women conceive. After the death rites at dusk, the chariot is considered a house of death, and the lifeless head is removed from the frame of its skeletal body, covered with a cloth and paraded around the village as though at a funeral. It is then taken to the temple of Kali, where it is revived. In a ceremony called the Natanam Thirumputhal—return dance—the head is once more taken around the village, right until the early hours of the morning. In the evening of the final day, a priest, representing Yudhishthira, crowns Aravan in a ceremony held in the inner sanctum of his temple.'

As the story seemed to wind to a close, the train also began to slow down. We could see yellow Indian Railways signs out of the windows indicating that the next stop was Viluppuram. We were all relieved to finally arrive in the little town, almost the last stop on our way to Koovagam. Our stiff limbs groaned as we stepped onto the platform: the sweet ache of movement after hours of confinement.

That familiar cocktail of emotions stirred again: terror swirling with joy. The old man walked out of the train and was nowhere to be seen, gone as surely as dust motes in the rays of the sun.

Exiting the station, we clambered onto a local bus packed with pilgrims and rumbled towards Viluppuram's main bus stop. 'The Koovagam celebrations happen at the Koothandavar temple,' a local on the bus explained, wiping the sweat off his face. 'Lord Aravan's shrine is about an hour from here.'

With that new information, it seemed as if a change of plans was imminent. I proposed that we check out the temple before setting our base somewhere. A recce is essential to my process.

'But wasn't the initial plan to book a room, freshen up and reach Koovagam before daylight vanishes?' replied Manu.

'Yes, but we should go to the temple first.'

'Why?'

நெடுஞ்சாலைத் துறை
குவாகம்
KOOVAGAM

'Sunset is approaching, and we should have a look at the temple, the surrounding areas and the locality before we start taking photos in earnest.'

A clearly unhappy Manu remained silent. And it was, paradoxically, because of this resistance, that I continued to insist on the new plan. I believe that the decisions that we make from that curious, unknowable blend of courage and madness can carry a person beyond what they believe are their limits. And so, with twilight darkening the skies, we agreed that the temple would be our starting point.

We soon boarded a local bus from Viluppuram, its seats worn smooth by generations of pilgrims, and rumbled into Manapattu, a tiny rail junction connecting to Koovagam. The bus dawdled to a halt in front of a tea shop where a few old men were seated outside.

We ordered some tea and approached the old men to ask about accommodations nearby. One of them replied, 'This is a remote village, there are almost no hotels here. You'll need to go back to Viluppuram.'

Time seemed to come to a standstill. Manu's gaze was fixed on the old men. When he turned to me, his eyes were blazing with anger. I forced a smile, playing a fool.

'Wipe that smile off your face and at least pretend to care,' he snapped.

Another old man leaned forward to ask if we were here for the festival, and we nodded. 'The real ceremonies only start tomorrow—you guys are quite early.'

Suddenly, Manu's irritation seemed to give way to curiosity. 'What happens tomorrow, ayya?' he asked.

The old man combed through his long, white beard with his fingers for a while and then began to elaborate. 'The priests conduct the wedding ceremonies, binding Lord Aravan and the aravanis in a sacred union, which is both commenced and ended within a single day. These aravanis, who have long been denied families of their own know at least this—for a few hours, they belong to someone and that someone belongs to them. You'll see what I mean tomorrow. Their joy cannot be expressed in mere words. They ache for what most of us take for granted: a home, children, the right to form roots and community without hiding.'

Manu and I, along with a few other bystanders, leaned in, listening attentively to the old man.

'Here at Koovagam, those who are afraid to reveal their true selves finally shed their masks. For eighteen nights, the thirunangai, transgender women, are accepted for who they are. Some pair off with men from the villages nearby like festival doves, others seek only drunken companionship, and still other want only sexual gratification. But very few people, if any at all, ask them their stories or actually try to understand them. The thirunangai have complete freedom here, and they reclaim their bodies and souls in evenings of wild revelry followed by wilder nights. Indeed, this is one of the most mysterious celebrations on Earth.'

I could already see it in my mind—the riot of colours, the pulsing music and beating drums, the pleasure of documenting unique stories. We thanked the old man for sharing his knowledge. His eyes crinkled as he left us with one final thought: 'Have a little faith. There's magic in the night, and if you only believe, you'll find magic everywhere.'

IN THE LAND OF MAGIC

30 APRIL

We left the tea shop and made our way to the dusty bus stand at Manapattu Junction. The orange-tinged dusk highlighted the parched paddy and sugarcane fields, gilding the backs of the workers going home after a long day. Minutes later, a minibus loaded with people lurched into view. Above the growl of the engine, the conductor's voice came through like a bell. 'Koovagam! Koovagam! KOOVAGAM!'

Each repetition sounded less like a destination and more like a summons.

'So, this is our passage to Koovagam,' I mused softly as our bus wound through a patchwork of emerald rice fields, towering coconut palms swaying on either side of the road. Everywhere I looked, the vegetation was as thick as a jungle, and the workers in the fields looked happy and healthy. As we approached the crest of a hill, we noticed an artificial lake surrounded by lovely gardens and electric fences. The edge of its dam glittered above a sea of sugarcane so vibrantly green that it hurt the eyes. *What a fertile land Koovagam is*, I thought to myself.

After a reflective silence between us, I asked Manu, 'Did you ever wonder, Manu, why that old man at the tea shop told us that there was magic in the night? That we'd be able to find it everywhere if we only looked? Do you think he says that to everyone he meets? Or perhaps he saw the spirits of curious seekers in us. Did you notice his face?' I asked.

'No,' he replied.

'He had a divine face and a truly peaceful smile.'

'I didn't have the time to notice his beautiful smile. I was a lot more worried about where we'd stay!' said Manu.

'That's right! We need to figure that soon—I think we should go to the temple and see if we can stay there tonight.'

Manu retreated into his watchful silence again.

A short while later, the bus made its final stop and we stepped out of it only to be jolted in shock. In every direction, all we could see was sugarcane, with no evidence of a temple or a festival.

Is this *Koovagam? Where is the temple?* I asked myself.

'You've arrived,' an old lady who was in the vicinity said meditatively in the local language, her voice dry, like fallen leaves rustling on the ground. 'Now help me with this basket.'

Manu and I looked at each other before jumping to assist her. As we hoisted the heavy basket and helped her balance it on her head, she studied us shrewdly. 'Are you going to Koothandavar kovil?'

'Yes, paati,' I replied, addressing her respectfully as grandmother.

'We have to walk through the sugarcane fields to reach Koothandavar temple—you can follow me,' she said.'

A few passengers from the bus were also planning to walk through the fields to Koovagam. As a group, we got off the main road and entered the sugarcane fields that unfolded like a green ocean, the fertility of the soil in this land on abundant display.

'Do you boys believe in god?' asked the old lady.

'Which god?' replied Manu.

'Gratitude is the compass that guides us home. No one gets very far if they forget who stood with them during tough times. God has his eyes fixed on his children and he will reward those who are kind and generous.' The old woman adjusted the basket perched on her head and continued, 'We will reach the temple soon if we take the shortcut, but remember, to experience god is to be united with him in all beings and in nature—this has been the journey of my life. And still, I walk.'

'Paati, shall we carry your basket for the rest of the way?' I asked.

'I never pass my burdens onto others' shoulders—I'm used to carrying this load.'

Our path took us to the edge of a tranquil field where the late evening sun was crowning over the tall ripple of the wild grass. Suddenly, without any warning, between these fields the silhouette of the temple suddenly appeared.

'Is that the Koothandavar kovil?' I asked the old lady.

'Yes, it is—this is where the whole event takes place.'

By the time we arrived at the temple, dusk had fallen and golden light from the temple flickered against the night. The old lady sat down in a small courtyard in front of the temple, her basket transforming into her shop. We had thought that the area might be empty at this in-between hour, but it buzzed with quiet industry: some locals were setting up their shops while a few policemen were doing their rounds. A small crowd of men and boys had begun to gather around the temple but we still had a clear view of the surroundings.

I noticed a man wearing bright clothes—vibhoothi neatly applied on his forehead—sitting outside the temple. The sacred ash on his forehead made from burnt wood and dried cow dung, spoke volumes. It was a quiet yet intense reminder that from dust we come and to dust we return. Nearby, transgender women drifted through the temple courtyard, their colourful saris swirling and their glass bangles clinking with each movement. Their laughter and joy seemed like a celebration of survival in a world that often pretends not to see them, or worse still, tries to erase them.

My heart began to beat faster—we had made it to Koovagam as planned. The irony wasn't lost on me: I was both my greatest cheerleader and my most vicious critic. Just hours earlier, I had been plagued with doubt: *Do I deserve to document these lives? Will they see my camera as just another outsider's gaze? Will they consider opening up to me?* But standing at the threshold of the temple, a new sense of purpose swept over me. I was glad that I had not let my insecurities and doubts dictate my decision. I understood in that moment that I was there, in Koovagam, for something much bigger than myself.

Standing next to me, Manu, however, still looked confused. We did not know where we were going to stay for the night, and this impulsive detour to the temple—instead of first securing accommodation—was clearly causing him great anxiety.

After wandering around the temple for a while, we came across a kaalaan, a small shack on one side of the road. As we were to find out later, the shop was owned by Subash anna and his wife. We needed locals to help us find a room for the night. And we were starving. So, we unloaded our bags at the shop and ordered a plate of mushroom masala while Manu searched online for hotels nearby.

Manu's agitation was palpable. And I empathized with him, too, really. We were carrying a lot of expensive paraphernalia and finding a secure base for the night was of utmost importance. While Manu looked online, I asked Subash anna, 'Where can we stay, anna?'

'Most of the transgender women and travellers who attend the festival stay at the locals' houses. Talk to the people around and if they find you genuine, you'll perhaps get a place to stay the night.'

'Subash anna's advice isn't ideal, but it is our only option,' Manu said, his fingers tightening around his camera bag. It was clear from Manu's expression that he was sceptical of this approach.

Each step we took here was a blind one. There were no maps, no guarantees. All we had was the terrifying, overwhelming freedom of the unknown. I finished the food on my plate, my eyes scanning the darkening spaces around us. After I had cleaned my hands, I slowly unzipped my camera bag, lifted out my camera and let its familiar weight anchor me to this moment of uncertainty.

'Look—the evening's festivities haven't even begun yet, Manu. Clear your mind of your worries. We came to capture magic, remember? Let's do that for a bit and once the function is over, we can travel back to Viluppuram if that's our last resort and find a place to stay there,' I said with more confidence than I was feeling.

'Okay, let's go then.'

And so, setting aside our worries, we moved towards the temple, cameras at the ready. As soon as we entered, we saw that the solemn wooden head of the idol of Lord Aravan was being raised on to a platform by a group of strong and well-built men, their bare chests gleaming with sweat, their biceps straining under the 25,000-kilogram weight of the idol distributed through a web of thick ropes. Others circled them, chanting encouragement:

'Aravan's strength flows through you!'

'The gods are pleased with your devotion!'

The men moved as if they had become a single unit; the statue rising inch by inch above the upturned faces of the crowd with each heave. Around us, the priests' sonorous mantras rose with the idol, each pull met with cries of 'Vel, vel Koothandavar!' and the air pulsed with the power of their faith.

Suddenly, a ceaseless firing of camera shutters and the mechanical whirring of zoom lenses replaced the chants. Bursts of artificial light painted the sweat-slicked devotees in stark relief. Out of nowhere, an arsenal of cameras had materialized, their glass eyes fixated on the spectacle, as if it were all a performance for their devices rather than a ritual of cultural significance. With a final heave, the middle portion of the idol was finally raised and tied to the base of the platform. The men erupted into joyful shouts.

Just then, I heard a woman's voice exclaim loudly, 'Otthu! Otthu! Move! Move!'

'*Vazhiya vittu Nagaru*! Get out of the way!'

I turned back to see who had spoken … There was a certain urgency in that command. In the haze of bodies around us, at first, I could not find at the woman who had spoken. She seemed to have blended into the crowd. But we were destined to meet her again, her part in our story was not yet over …

THE SUDDEN BLAZE OF A FLASH

30 APRIL

My eyes traced the direction from which the nearest camera was piercing the darkness of the night. A short, middle-aged lady wearing a black kurta was taking pictures of some trans women. As soon as she had finished with the task, they surrounded her and demanded money.

The woman sternly responded, 'Why should I give you any money? Mudiyathu. I won't.'

Manu and I edged closer, our cameras in our hands, observing the confrontation. The trans women persisted in their demands, but the other woman, too, stood her ground. One of trans women complained to another, 'Just look at the way she talks to us!'

'All right, fine. Don't give us any cash, but at least show us our pictures,' said another.

As the woman scrolled through her camera roll with them, Manu's shutter clicked and captured the candid moment. That picture would prove to be the key to getting ourselves a place to stay that night, as we found out later.

'Let's go talk to her, Manu,' I said.

We moved closer to attempt a conversation, and though the woman noticed us as we approached, she only smiled and continued to click more pictures.

While we were considering what to do, the festival continued to unfold around us at an ever-increasing pace, each moment demanding that we document it. Putting aside the idea of striking a conversation with the woman for the moment, Manu chased the action shots as I looked for faces for portraits. I prefer portraiture because that's the best way to capture the personality, essence and raw emotions of a person. While taking portraits, the atmosphere is extremely important because it isn't merely a setting—it helps reveal the subject's inner world. As a photographer, I tend to wait for various elements to align—place, light and truth—before I ever release my shutter.

As I would realize later, my favourite images from the festival were of the intimate rituals of the trans women we had met—lovingly fixing each other's jewellery and saris, sharing a meal, shopping together for wares ...

As Manu and I continued to shoot, each drawn by different instincts and rhythms, we witnessed something rather unexpected. A few men were tying thalis not only to transgender women but also to other men.

Just as I was wondering what that might signify, a familiar voice spoke from behind me, 'This as well is a practice that has traditionally been part of the event and it stems from popular beliefs prevailing in the community. Elderly men who have taken certain vows and pledged service to the god Koothandavar, tie thalis to each other, usually when these vows are fulfilled.'

I turned to see the woman in the black kurta standing behind me.

'Oh, really? That's so strange.'

'Is this your first time here?'

'Yes.'

'Then many more adventures await you tomorrow.'

As she spoke, she relaxed a little and smiled. Eventually, we struck a deeper conversation with her, and we found out more about her. Her name was Madhu, and she was attending the festival for the fifth time. There was another woman who accompanied her—a local—Chinna Ponnu, a guide who had been born and raised in Viluppuram and knew all the intricacies and historical details of the event.

A casual conversation seemed to have brought us all together momentarily: a group of photographers in a remote Indian village, witnessing and documenting one of the most transformative experiences of our lives. Manu quickly pulled out his camera and showed Madhu the photo he'd taken of her, capturing the moment the transgender women had playfully demanded money from her. She was rather impressed to see it.

She went on to tell us about her own experiences at the festival in the past. 'The more I visit this place, the more I learn about the transgender community and their history with this festival. I meet a lot of passionate and curious photographers, travellers and journalists every year.'

'Can you tell us what you know about the Koovagam festival?' I asked her.

'Sure, many others have asked me the same question. Even though it seems that much is already known about the festival and its rituals, there are things that we still don't know. Some make fun of these myths and practices, while others take time to understand them.'

Manu drew closer, looking interested.

'On the full moon day of the Chithirai month of the Tamil calendar every year, transgender people from all over India gather at this temple in Koovagam to celebrate their wedding to Lord Koothandavar, who is also known as Aravan.'

'Why is he known as Aravan? Also, why do they marry Koothandavar and not any other god?' asked Manu.

'Aravan is a minor character in the Mahabharata, the son of the Pandava prince Arjuna and the Naga princess Uloopi. At the Koovagam festival, the transgenders and transvestites are considered the wives of Aravan, which, as you might be able to guess, is where the term "aravani" comes from. Here, the aravanis first marry Lord Aravan—who also came to be known as Koothandavar—and revel in their joy of being married, tying thalis around their necks and wearing colourful bangles on the first night. But as the procession of Aravan goes through the village the next day, the brides break their thalis and bangles and mourn their widowhood through ritualistic dancing: this whole cycle re-enacts the ancient story of Aravan's sacrifice during the Kurukshetra war.'

'Oh!' Manu exclaimed.

'It is believed that before he sacrificed himself for the greater good of the Pandavas, Aravan wanted to be married. So, Krishna married Aravan by taking the form of a woman named Mohini; the only female avatar of his original form of Vishnu.'

'Really?' exclaimed Manu.

'There are also various other interesting beliefs and myths associated with the festival, such as how Koothandavar blesses childless women with the ability to conceive.'

'Fascinating,' I responded. 'I read online that a beauty pageant is also held during the festival every year?'

'Yes,' she nodded. 'Doctors, older trans women and NGOs come together to discuss transgender rights and raise awareness about sexual health issues related to the community.'

'That's amazing,' Manu said. 'Koovagam is truly enchanting, almost like an alien world.'

At that, I noticed a shift in Madhu's demeanour as she grew a bit agitated.

'No, it is not an alien world; it is the eunuch's pocket-sized universe. It is because of them that the cultural essence of this land is kept alive. They gather here for eighteen days, breathing life into an otherwise lifeless, forgotten village,' she said, her tone sharp. 'Tell me, have you read the Mahabharata?'

We nodded in unison.

'Well, the Koovagam festival has its roots in the Kurukshetra war; Krishna's cunning and the noble nature of a very valiant young man are the basis of this festival.'

By this time, the men who had lifted the idol had gone home, and only the four of us seemed to be around. As the night deepened, it became darker and breezier. Madhu had a lot to share about Koovagam, the community and their cultural beliefs, but she felt it was not safe to linger in the open once the crowds had dissipated. Though she had first seemed intimidating and commanding, she turned out to be quite generous and friendly. Noticing that we had no clue about where we would stay, Chinna Ponnu leaned in and whispered to Madhu, who, in turn, made us an offer we couldn't refuse.

'I am expecting a friend to arrive today, but he may not be here anytime soon. In fact, I don't think he will make it tonight. If you are comfortable, you can stay in the room we'd reserved for him in our guest house.'

Tears of joy filled our eyes and our hearts were overwhelmed with gratitude. Without a second thought, we accepted the generous proposal.

'Come to the Chengalrayan Mills by 10 p.m.,' she said. 'It is about 5 kilometres from here. Wait by the entrance and call me. I shall make the required arrangements before you arrive,' she said, handing us her contact number before leaving.

I stood there, a little stunned by her kindness and thought to myself: *When it rains, it pours.*

I was at once thirsty, exhausted and exhilarated as I strode out of the temple area. A few remaining street vendors were starting to leave as well. Manu and I began to walk back through the sugarcane fields. Suddenly, he turned around and smiled broadly, the immensity of the festival registering itself in his mind.

'This is a miracle. I never thought the woman who seemed so brusque would offer us a place to stay,' said Manu.

'Do you think it's wise to accept her offer, though? Do you think it'll be safe?'

'Honestly, I was also thinking about it.'

'But then, what is the other option, Manu? I think we should remember what the old man at Manapattu Junction told us: Let's show a little faith and we will find some magic in the night. And if we truly believe, there will be magic everywhere.'

Manu laughed, and a heartbeat later, I joined in. It was getting late, and we made our way towards the main road.

As we got there, Manu saw some men standing under a streetlight. 'Anna, how do we get to Chengalrayan Mills right now?' he asked one of them.

'All the buses have left, but there is an autorickshaw stand at the end of the road. You'll be able to get shared autos there,' the man replied.

We thanked him and began walking towards the auto stand. Within minutes, we'd bought two seats on the next shared auto that was leaving for Viluppuram. After about fifteen minutes, we were dropped off in front of the isolated Chengalrayan Mills. Though the road looked like a national highway, it was eerily quiet, with barely a vehicle in sight.

'Let's call her,' said Manu.

It was almost 10 p.m. The call disconnected right after the first ring, and the second time I tried, it beeped for a bit and then dropped again.

'Try again in a while,' Manu said.

I did, but the third call ended the same way. We could do nothing but wait.

Within minutes, I could sense that Manu was seething again. He sat down on a milestone and deposited his luggage on the road. I joined him. The darkness stretched on.

An hour passed. 'Perhaps we should look for an alternative,' I said.

He didn't respond immediately, and after what seemed like an eternity, he said, 'I don't think people use this road often. Nor do I think it's safe to stay here indefinitely. Let's give it another few minutes, now that we have waited so long, but if there's no development, we must make a move.'

Just then, almost as if we had conjured it with our desperation, we saw a bike heading towards us. It slowed to a stop at the gate. The two men on it were in security uniforms. The person sitting at the back got off first and stared directly at us for a minute. Then he pulled out his phone and made a call. After a short pause, he walked up to us and handed over his phone, his sharp eyes fixed on me. Not knowing what else to do, I took the phone.

'Hello?'

'These security guards will guide you to the guest house. Go with them.'

It was Madhu. I breathed a deep sigh of relief. I have always believed that travel isn't about getting from one place to another, it's about allowing yourself to be profoundly changed by the world. And so often, it's the small acts of kindness—towards strangers and people we love—that can impact us in the most moving ways.

We entered the gates of the compound, escorted by the two men, and walked down a lane that took us deeper into the heart of this mysterious estate. A few minutes later, we found ourselves standing outside an old house. Madhu was still dressed in her black kurta when she came outside to greet us. 'I have asked security to clean the room.' After a small pause, she said, 'The guest house is a bit isolated but it's hardly a few minutes' walk away. Do you mind sleeping alone? Do you guys need security?'

'No, thank you. We can take care of ourselves,' I said.

'You know the place has not been used for a while now, and I'd rather ensure your safety,' she said. 'Rajendran,' she called loudly, and a security guard appeared from inside the house. 'Tonight, you must stay with these two boys at our guest house.'

The thin old man nodded and took the keys from her.

We took our leave promptly, the exhaustion of the day taking its toll on us. Rajendran anna switched on a torch and led the way for us. We strolled towards the guest house on a concrete path flanked by dense trees. He opened the main door and showed us into a spacious room. 'Is this room all right with you?' he asked.

Both Manu and I were shocked to see the well-maintained, air-conditioned bedroom. 'It is more than what we deserve,' I said in a humble tone.

'If there is an emergency, just call me, and I'll be right here,' Rajendran anna said as he stepped out of the room.

Manu took his clothes and towel out of his bag and said, 'I'm going to take a shower.'

I settled into the comfortable bed and thought about the day we had had. *There is certainly magic in this world*, I told myself.

A SHORT HISTORY OF KOOVAGAM

1 MAY

By the time Manu was done, it was midnight. We stepped outside for a smoke. As Manu was about to light his cigarette, Rajendran anna arrived, looking at us with a steady, suspicious gaze. We quickly tried to hide our cigarettes, unsure if smoking in front of him was appropriate.

Hoping to alleviate the tension, I pointed to a photo frame in the hallway and asked, 'Who is the man in the picture, Rajendran anna?'

'That's Chengalrayan ayya. He built everything you see here. In the 1980s, this place was nothing but dry land with a few families and houses. At that time, Koovagam was a remote village that the government did not bother about. Then the sugar mills began to operate and the locals, both men and women, found jobs. After the harvest season, ayya built roads to improve transport, expanded the mills, and set up schools, hospitals and temples across a 250-acre stretch.'

'Seriously? Across 250 acres of land?' I asked, shocked.

'Do you remember the entrance sign for Chengalrayan Mills?'

'Yes.'

'From there to here—that's all of it. However, only the schools are functioning now.'

A few minutes passed in silence and then with a spark of sudden energy, Rajendran anna pulled out his old Nokia phone and quickly browsed through it. His face lit up when he found what he was looking for and he excitedly asked, 'Have you heard villu pattu?'

'No, what's that, anna?' I asked.

'Well, villu pattu, or the bow song, is not simply entertainment—it is our culture, our history. In the villages of Tamil Nadu, performers use it to narrate stories from mythology and even contemporary social issues. Here, the main storyteller strikes the villu, the bow, which rests on an inverted mud pot. With each strike, the story unfolds further. A co-performer beats the pot in time with the strikes of the bow.'

There was something reverential in the way he described this art form, like he was speaking of a sacred ritual rather than just a song.

'Sometimes, even the local government uses this art form to spread social messages—or propaganda. This unique method of storytelling is folklore at its best. Here, listen to this telling of the legend of Aravan!'

Manu and I sat up almost instantly, curious like two beginners at a consecrated initiation, and waited for the villu pattu version of Lord Aravan's story to play on Rajendran anna's phone.

In a few seconds, a burst of folk music rose up as a vibrant male voice started narrating the ancient epic. Rajendran anna placed his phone on the table right in front of us and closed his eyes. Manu sat next to me, looking at the phone with interest.

The music surged, followed by a deep, rhythmic voice greeting the listeners before launching into the main narrative.

And then began the villu pattu performance in earnest.

'Years ago, a war between the Pandavas and Kauravas was imminent and inevitable. Krishna, the protector of the universe, was worried about its outcome. He could intervene using his divine powers, but the warriors were required to decide their own fate. Yet, he wanted the Pandavas to win the war as he thought their deeds were just and moral,' cried the storyteller.

'Oho! So, the god himself was biased,' asked a group of listeners.

'Maybe he was, maybe he wasn't—or maybe he just believed in fairness. If things had gone the way he hoped, it would have been the perfect good-overcomes-evil story.

'And so, having no choice, Krishna went to Sahadeva, who had the gift of prophecy and telling the future, but to his great surprise and dismay, he found Duryodhana there.'

'Oho!' sighed the crowd followed by a few loud, but incomprehensible whispers.

"Welcome, my lords!" exclaimed Sahadeva. "How may I help you both?"

'Presenting his request, Duryodhana said, "O Madriputra, being true to your skill, guide me such that I can claim victory in the upcoming war."

'Nodding thoughtfully, Sahadeva looked at Krishna and asked, "And what I can do for you, my lord?"

"Sahadeva, I came to ask the same favour for the Pandavas."

'Without saying a word, Sahadeva rolled his prediction shells, made a few mental calculations, and then looked up at his guests. "The path to victory is similar for the both of you," he explained. "To win the war, you must offer a sacrifice to the goddess of war, Kali—a man who possesses valour, strength, beauty and bravery. Whoever performs this sacrifice first will receive Kali's blessings and triumph," said Sahadeva as he looked at Krishna with worried eyes.

'"Leave that to me, Sahadeva," said Krishna and left. On his way back, all he could think of was who might end up victorious. He could only think of only two people who could satisfy the criteria required for the sacrifice—himself and Arjuna. And neither could be given up.'

'Oh no! Adadei! What did Krishna do next? asked a man from the audience.'

Just then, Manu's phone rang. He pulled it out of his pocket and walked over to the far end of the fence, which until then had been veiled in darkness. Rajendran anna immediately paused the performance on his phone.

'Thank you for sharing this with us, anna' I said.

'That's all right,' said Rajendran anna. 'I usually tell these stories to everyone who visits for the Koovagam festival. As you know, some stories need to be shared with the outer world, whereas some need to be hidden.'

Manu soon rejoined the conversation. 'Sorry about that,' he said. 'That was a call from another photographer for a job.'

'Oh. Well, shall I continue or do you guys want to go to sleep?' asked Rajendran anna.

Before I could speak, Manu intervened and said, 'No, no! Please continue with the play—we are very interested in hearing the rest of it.'

Rajendran anna took a deep breath, smiled and resumed playing the clip. The narrator's voice boomed out of the tinny phone speaker once again:

'With a heavy heart, Krishna shared Sahadeva's predictions with the Pandavas. "Is there anyone, anyone except Arjuna, who matches all the requirements for the sacrifice? Anyone at all?"

'He pleaded for other ideas, only to be met by a stunned silence. His heart shattered at the thought of losing a dear friend. He began to feel discomforted when he heard a voice ask, "Am I eligible to be sacrificed?"

'Krishna turned to see who had spoken. It was a very handsome warrior bearing a striking resemblance to Arjuna. "Who are you, child?" asked Krishna, hope slowly reviving in his heart.

'"I am Aravan, son of Arjuna and Uloopi, the princess of the Nagas. I'm here to help my father and his brothers win the war," he said. "And if my life is what it takes to help them succeed, I am ready to make that sacrifice," he said.

'Krishna felt a wave of relief. Using his divine powers, he confirmed that

Aravan was indeed a truly exceptional warrior with remarkable strength, character and courage. He knew instantly that Aravan would make the perfect sacrifice for Kali. Krishna asked Aravan to follow him and introduced him to the Pandavas, including his father, Arjuna. He spoke highly of Aravan, praising his noble qualities and his willingness to make the ultimate sacrifice.

'"You will be sacrificed to the goddess at dawn tomorrow. Purify yourself mentally and physically and prepare for the day. Long live your sacrifice!" cried Krishna.'

A loud round of applause erupted through the phone's speaker, even though it seemed clear that the audience was grappling with mixed emotions about the unfolding plot.

'Aravan had one last wish to fulfil before he sacrificed his life—he wanted to die a married man. However, it was impossible to find a woman willing to be married only for a day and live the life of a widow immediately after. And so, Lord Krishna assumed the form of Mohini, his only female avatar, and married Aravan, allowing him to enjoy one day of marital happiness. The following day, Aravan was beheaded and sacrificed to the goddess Kali. Mohini was devastated by her grief and intensely mourned his death.'

With that, the villu pattu came to an end. I checked the time: 1.30 a.m. Manu and I waited to see if Rajendran anna had anything more to tell us.

Sensing our interest, Rajendran anna continued, 'These days, the number of artists engaging in villu pattu has decreased tremendously because their income from these performances is only enough for a hand-to-mouth existence. The story you heard may perhaps be a myth, but the transgender community in India consider themselves to be Mohini, and they celebrate the Koothandavar festival in memory of this incident every year. Did you notice the wooden head of Aravan at the temple?'

'Yes, we were there when it was being raised on to the platform,' Manu said.

'On the seventeenth day, the priests at the Koothandavar temple perform matrimonial rituals by reciting mantras and decorating Aravan's idol with garlands and tying a thali around the necks of all the aravanis.'

'Will that happen tomorrow?'

'Yes, and once it does, they will become the wives of Aravan, and they will spend all night merrymaking, dancing and singing. Heavy rains and thunderstorms are usually expected on the night of the wedding ritual.'

'Are you saying there will be rain tomorrow?' Manu asked, sceptical of these weather predictions.

I was also a little doubtful because I remembered that when we'd reached the railway station in the morning, we were extremely thirsty because of the heat and humidity. Indeed, the chances of rain seemed bleak.

'Of course! Our Koothandavar will bless us with rain,' Rajendran anna said confidently. 'And then, at dawn the next day, the aravanis will rip the yellow string off their necks and cry loudly, beating their chests with both hands and rolling on the floor, following an ancient mourning ritual reminiscent of how Mohini grieved Aravan's death. Following this, they bathe in the Varaha river, which runs by the temple, and then dress in white to symbolize their widowhood.'

'Remarkable!' said Manu.

'It's something that feels like a revelation,' Rajendran anna replied. 'Or a sudden longing to understand, all at once, the laws of this world—its beauty and harshness, its kindness and cruelty, its vastness and reality. It's a special experience, one that can't be explained in words. It *needs* to be witnessed and experienced. But it is very late now, and you guys must sleep. Madhu madam has instructed me to wake you up by 6.30 a.m.'

Rajendran anna left, blowing his whistle and shining his flashlight in every direction to ensure that there were no trespassers or animals around.

PART 2

FOLKLORE

1 MAY

When I opened my eyes in the morning—far sooner than I would've liked—bright sunlight was streaming through the window.

I quickly got out of bed, went through my morning ablutions and dressed in my favourite cargo pants, which had way more pockets than I thought I would require. When we left our room, Chinna Ponnu was waiting for us at the entrance of the guest house with a basket and a banana leaf.

'Breakfast!' she said as she handed the food over to us with a pleasant smile.

The basket contained a silver tin full of idlis, a small box of podi and a container of oil. The taste of the podi idlis blended with the fragrance of the banana leaf was truly divine. Once we had finished eating, we returned the basket to Chinna Ponnu and packed our bags to head out for the day.

On our way to Koovagam, Manu remained distracted, his fingers drumming restlessly against his camera bag. Perhaps, like me, he was also thinking about how he should carry himself in a space largely reserved as a haven for members of the transgender community. Truth be told, I had no idea how to navigate it either. We were stepping into a world with its own codes, both spoken and unspoken, where our well-intentioned curiosity might still feel like intrusion and appropriation.

We reached the temple and spent some taking it all in. Groups of trans women were arriving in increasing numbers, some walking in lively clusters, others arriving in vans, their laughter ringing in the sunshine. Their excitement seemed to make the air crackle.

A few groups of local men and self-styled roadside Romeos loitered around these groups, hunting for the most beautiful aravanis to flirt with. Nearby, bangles and thalis glittered in makeshift stalls, selling out almost as fast as they were put on display. Fruit sellers wandered through the crowd, their baskets balanced delicately on their heads, while the food stalls were packed, the fragrance of fried food hanging heavy in the air.

We moved towards the Koothandavar temple, its gopurams rising high above the hectic activities of its devotees. There were two entrances stood before us: a main gate that was thronging with devotees, and a VIP entrance that was well-guarded and quieter. Police officers patrolled nearby.

A tangibly vivacious energy, laughter, music, the clinking of bangles suffused everything around us … I was elated to be in Koovagam.

While Manu and I were both giddy with joy to see the activity around us, we were also deeply conscious about the correct manner in which we could approach the transgender women to click their photos and talk to them about their life stories.

'Manu, let's go talk to the women bathing in the pond.'

'What? No! That's the worst idea ever. They'll think we're harassing them,' said Manu.

I immediately realized how silly the idea sounded. It wasn't okay to approach women during such a private moment, camera in hand, like an insensitive voyeur. But something inexplicable pushed my feet towards the pond against my better judgement.

When the women saw me walking towards them with my camera, I sensed a sharp uneasiness among them. Using my most respectful tone, I asked one woman sitting by the steps of the ponds, 'Akka, ungala oru photo eduthukava? May I click a picture of you?'

'Entha channel, tambi? Which television channel do you work for?' she asked.

'We are not from the media.'

'Then take as many as you please.'

Her eyes lingered on me for a second before she broke into a warm smile. We guided her through a few poses and took a few pictures. As I thanked her for being so gracious, I quickly reviewed the shots. While one part of me was delighted that our first interaction had turned out so well, another winced at the mediocre lighting and composition of the photos.

'Look here, tambi!' a voice rang out happily. 'I have longer hair and bigger breasts. Take my picture too!' shouted another transgender woman, striking a dramatic pose. We were surprised by their boldness at first but equally grateful to be invited into the group so warmly.

Later, while I was browsing through the photos we had taken, I felt a quiet satisfaction. Each frame was a beautiful blend of emotions, of bonds, of fleeting moments, of life in its most unfiltered form. There was colour, there was chaos, but most of all, there was truth etched into every smile, every embrace, every twinkle in every eye.

'Akka,' I ventured, leaning forward from my perch on the steps, watching the morning light dance over the pond's surface, 'could you share your story with us? What first made you realize you were transgender? How did this journey begin?'

One woman, her bangles clinking softly as she adjusted her sari, listened intently to my question, considered it for a moment and then began her tale. 'Growing up, I was never just one thing—I was not always a tomboy, nor was I always very feminine. Sometimes I enjoyed how my mother dressed me up in lacy dresses and sometimes I thought those were the worst of my clothes. Sometimes, I played with dolls and sometimes, my brother's cars were more fun. In those days, we didn't know there was anything beyond being a "boy" or a "girl". To our families, anything different was . . . unthinkable. I hated puberty because suddenly my body seemed completely foreign. I could barely stand to look in the mirror since what looked back at me didn't feel at all right. I told myself it was all normal, that everyone around me was feeling this disconnect with their body. But the truth kept gnawing at me.'

Another woman, seeming almost shocked that someone had asked these questions to one of her sisters, interrupted. 'I was depressed for most of my teenage years and I frequently thought about taking my own life. During these years, I also doubted my faith constantly—how could I love the god who made me when I couldn't be content with the form he had given me? It was only in the third year of college, when I transferred to an art school, that I finally learned about the questions I had never known to ask. Three years have passed since then, and I am still coming to terms with who I am. Because you see, in a way, it's hard for me to understand and explain. Some days I am male, some days I am female, some days I am neither—and some days I am both. And despite knowing who I am now, there is still fear. I fear how the people I love will react, they who have never treated the transgender community with any grace but only scorn, pity or mockery. I fear exposing myself to their reactions because I believe I will be rejected, and I cannot survive their rejection,' she said, pain and anger echoing in her voice. 'A major turning point for me, though, was meeting a doctor through a friend and undergoing surgery.'

'How did you feel after the surgery? What was the whole process like, akka?' Manu asked.

'During college, it felt as if my life was at a standstill. I couldn't work out, dance or really do anything in the way I wanted. So, I talked it over with a friend, Malar, and decided that it was time to explore gender-affirmation surgery. Luckily, not long after I

பேஷன்
Fashion

applied for an appointment, a doctor from Chennai called me and I immediately went to meet her. She told me she would love to do my surgery, and by some quirk of fate, the first available date was 4 June, the day after my nineteenth birthday. That sunrise didn't just mark a new day—it became the day of my second birth, when I finally emerged as my true self.'

'Was the procedure painful? How did you manage it all alone?' I asked as the others remained silent, moved by her story.

'Well, with a little more than five months to go before the surgery, there were still a few essential procedures I had to get done; which were the most painful, but in retrospect, they were worth it. One of the most difficult ones was the electrolysis on the genital area for hair removal—even the needle for the anaesthetic caused excruciating pain. In those moments, as I screamed through the pain, I would steady myself by saying, "I'm going to have a vagina at the end of this." I have never once doubted my decision, not even during the worst parts of the healing process. Recovering from surgery, especially the process of dilation, was painful and uncomfortable, and to be honest, it sometimes still is. After the first year, experts recommend dilating twice a week, or having sex often, to ensure that the depth and width of the vagina are maintained. Though really, plenty of cisgender women need to dilate as well and it's more common than you might think!' she finished, laughing at my surprise.

'After a summer of recovery, I returned to my hometown, ready to be my true self. However, the pain didn't subside until a full year after surgery. I would experience sharp, quick, sporadic pains in my vagina. I often felt like there was an electric shock running through my clitoris, but that only meant that my nerve endings were beginning to function again. After about a year, I was fully healed, and this is where I think the medical transition process ends. Having a vagina was how I felt "complete" in my body but let me be clear: surgery isn't a requirement for being transgender. Today, a lot has changed for the better, and medicine has made huge strides since I started to transition. Now, many of the processes that I went through have become simpler and more streamlined.'

'Nandri, akka, thank you,' I said, my heart brimming with vulnerability and tenderness.

Live Your Dreams

(An ISO 9000-2001 Certified Institution)
VILLUPURAM

ENTERING THE KOOTHANDAVAR TEMPLE

1 MAY

When Manu and I walked towards the temple a little later, we could see that the grounds were buzzing with activity: droves of trans women, dressed in their finest clothes and jewellery were busy talking to each other and preparing for the main event of the day—the thali ceremony. Some were accompanied by their partners and some others had arrived in groups. Almost all of them bought malli poo, or jasmine flowers, thalis and coconuts from the vendors outside the temple, adding more oomph to their appearance. I scanned the crowd for the most striking faces for portrait shots, and when I found someone, I rushed to capture her face with my lens.

Just then, another trans woman passing by asked to see my pictures. She scrolled through them with interest and then shook my hand. 'Nice pictures and a great smile,' she said huskily as her ring finger caressed my inner palm.

'Thanks, akka,' I replied, giving her a sincere smile.

She paused, her face softening for a moment and then replied, 'Seri, all right, tambi. Whenever you find time, come take pictures of me inside the temple, okay?'

I smiled and nodded in agreement. As I was making my way to the temple, I spotted Madhu and Chinna Ponnu standing in line to get a glimpse of Koothandavar's idol. I joined them. We entered the cramped inner sanctum and saw an old priest tying thalis around the necks of children, adult men and trans women. The temple staff moved quickly, tying one knot after another with practised rhythm. Some trans women were even marrying the men they had come with.

I had not noticed until then, but suddenly, in the crowd, I realized that Manu was nowhere to be seen. *He will have to wait now to be found*, I thought. I was mesmerized by the red-headed Koothandavar in front of me, the face made fierce by intense, bulging eyes and a huge, exaggerated moustache. Only the deity's head was enshrined and worshipped in the temple, a visceral reminder of his mythic sacrifice. When we reached the front of the queue, a priest applied vibhuti and kumkumam pottu (a vermillion mark) on our foreheads.

BUYING A THALI

A stream of trans women was exiting through the main sanctum, thalis tied around their necks, looking extremely happy because they were 'officially' married now. Each face glowed brighter than the temple lamps—these were not just ornaments but hard-won badges of legitimacy. Once the previous groups had exited, others entered the complex after them to partake in the same joy.

As we walked out of the temple, I saw that Manu was waiting at the entrance. Around us, transgender women were efficiently distributing food and water, and Chinna Ponnu went to bring us all some refreshments.

The heat was becoming unbearable now, as the sun climbed high up in the sky and became harsh. People were finding shelter under the scattered shade of trees, fanning themselves, hunting for whatever relief they could manage.

'It is really hot today,' said Madhu. 'I should have brought a cap at the very least.'

Reaching into my backpack, I pulled out a dupatta, one that belonged to my mother, and gave it to her. It was soft with age and, to my mind at least, smelled like amma. I tend to carry it on shoots or when I travel, because when I feel homesick or am reminded of my mother, I take it out and hold on to it as if I am holding on to her, as if she's right there next to me.

'Do you have one for yourself?'

'I do,' I lied innocently, even though I didn't have another. I wanted to give our gracious host something in return for the help she had offered us the previous night.

She smiled and took it from me. We sat in the temple veranda, waiting for the heat to subside. As we watched the crowd grow denser near the temple gates, Madhu began to speak.

'There is a lot of confusion about transgender, transsexual and intersex identities. There are similarities, no doubt, but there are also too many differences to dismiss and club them all together. Some people decide to change or affirm their genders surgically, after identifying their individual conditions. This decision is often inspired by a kind of a hormonal disorder, which varies from person to person.'

She paused, watching a group of trans women walk by, their faces radiant with mirth. 'This festival celebrating the trans community is one of the biggest in Asia and indeed is an eye-opener for all of us. The truth is that a vast number of people with intersex conditions identify as male or female rather than as transgender or transsexual. Common to all these groups, however, is a dreadful sense of alienation that they feel in society, even as they deal with so much emotional turmoil in their personal lives and within their bodies. Koovagam allows them to find a community where they can truly belong. For many transgender women, this festival is so hugely significant because it is their only chance to get married. Across the country, transgender individuals are looked down upon because of their sexuality, and most are forced into prostitution to make a living. Although some states in India, most notably Tamil Nadu and Kerala, have legislated measures for transgender inclusion, much remains to be done still. Festivals like Koovagam that give hope not just to the transgender community but also send out a message to all of us in general to be more accepting of our differences,' she finished meditatively.

While she was talking, I noticed an elderly woman bow reverentially in front of a transgender devotee, so I asked Madhu about it. 'Why do people seek blessings from members of the transgender community?'

'They are devotees of Lord Krishna and are considered living embodiments of his grace. Thus, when they bless you, it is god's own favour that you receive. They have also had a prominent role in arts and entertainment and were honoured in royal

courts. During the Mughal era, they played a seminal role in training children of the court in royal manners and etiquette,' she responded.

Madhu continued, 'Members of the larger community are known by various names, but there are differences within the sub groups, too, undoubtedly. The hijra communities in India, for example, are very diverse: they mostly consist of transgender women but include intersex and non-binary individuals as well. It may also be argued that hijras are one of the more well-known sub groups and are revered in the country. Most of them cannot have children. Others may not have the ability to have children at all. Most people in the hijra communities have faced rejection all their lives; they were thrown out of their homes by their own parents in many cases and know no family other than each other. For many, the concept of "family", really, begins amongst this community that they build with each other.

She chose her next words carefully. 'India, a feminine male who takes a receptive role during sex with a man will often identify as a kothi. While kothis are usually distinguished from hijras as a separate gender identity, they often dress as women and act in a feminine manner in public spaces, even using feminine vocabulary or pronouns to refer to themselves, as hijras do. For both hijras and kothis, their usual partners are cisgender men as they can engage in penetrative sex. These male partners are often married to cisgender women and any relationships of this nature are usually kept secret from their own families. Some hijras may form relationships with men and even marry, although their marriages are not recognized by law or religion. Hijras and kothis have a name for these masculine sexual or romantic partner as well. They call them panthi.'

Here, she paused for a minute and then said, 'These gender identities go far beyond Western labels, Shino. Unlike labels such as gay, lesbian or bisexual, which describe sexual orientation, the labels we are talking about include complex gender roles, social presentation and preference of sexual position as well. It's a broader, more layered framework built through centuries of tradition and communal codes of belonging. For these individuals, adopting intersex or transgender kids can present an opportunity that most desire with all their hearts—to have someone they can call their own.'

Madhu then shared some stories that have remained with me until this day. She told me about a thirty-six-year-old transgender woman, an AIDS awareness social worker, who had chosen her first name, Rangeela, from the title of the popular Hindi film; in a symbolic act of reinvention. She came to Koovagam each year with her 'clan' of informally adopted transgender daughters—Tamizh, Reena, Malar and Aarti—who were all between fifteen and twenty-three years of age.

These women preferred to use only their first names, female names they had chosen with pride and intention, and deliberately abjure their last names because of their desire to leave their past lives behind. They travelled nine hours by bus from Tuticorin on the coast of Tamil Nadu to Koovagam, carrying with their strength and resilience, the unshakeable belief that this space was not only one of belonging but also of healing for them.

Rangeela, who had been attending the festival for the last seven years, first arrived as a transitioning cross-dresser dabbling in sex work. Madhu told us that Rangeela was now a fully transitioned woman and served as guru to the young girls in her neighbourhood. Tamizh, who came from the nearby village of Vilathikulam, was considered the 'pretty one' because of her soft, feminine appearance. Rangeela took her in permanently when Tamizh consumed a bottle of hair dye in an attempt to die by suicide after her lover left her for another transgender girl the year before. Her daughter Reena, tall and voluptuous with a loud personality, had transitioned in 2006 at the age of fifteen.

Then there was Malar, just a year younger than Tamizh, and

her cousin by birth. Their families were so close that as children they had addressed each other as 'brother'. Now they called each other 'sister'. It's a quiet but powerful shift, reflecting the profound change of identity that the Koovagam celebrates. Finally, Madhu talked about Aarti, the youngest at sixteen, who had been transitioning for only three months. Her young age, however, didn't stop her from winning a minor beauty pageant in Koovagam that was sponsored by a state-run AIDS organization.

As I listened to these stories of trans families, I was incredibly moved. Each woman, scarred, resilient and beautiful, forced me to confront how little I understood about the price of becoming yourself and owning your story in a world that constantly denies you the right to exist.

'I'd once asked Rangeela why she came here often, and she replied, "This is where our larger family, our community, comes to reunite. This is the one place where we can worship without being whispered about, where my girls see others like themselves thriving and have hope for their futures." That helped me see things completely differently' Madhu said, completing the saga of Rangeela's family.

'It doesn't make sense to me. Society pushes trans women into oppressive professions and then chastises them for it. Sex work is such an ancient part of our culture, then why is there such stigma around it, especially when it concerns trans women?'

Madhu nodded. 'I don't have an answer for you, Shino. The district where Rangeela and her daughters live is home to roughly fifty transgender women, are three hundred or so if you include the surrounding villages. Her house, located in a quiet, shady lane ten minutes from the Tuticorin harbour, is a cross between a family home and a boarding house. The rent is 8,000 rupees per month. Rangeela's monthly salary at Alliance, a non-profit focused on HIV/AIDS awareness and advocacy, is 5,000 rupees. I'm sure you can already see how hard her life must be. The rest of the rent, along with groceries, water and fuel for her scooter, is paid for by the women who live with her. Each is expected to contribute 200 rupees daily whether through collection, begging or sex work. In exchange, they are given food, shelter and emotional support during their transition into womanhood.'

'But our temples enshrine transgender deities who are forms of our most powerful gods. Just look at Ardhanarishwara, the half-male, half-female Shiva! People will bow to these forms but condemn the living embodiments of that same divinity?' I protested.

Madhu had a sad smile on her face. 'Again, I don't know what to say, Shino. We worship gods who transcend form yet insist on denying that gender exists outside the two binaries—and this contradiction plays out on the streets every day. As you know, these women support themselves through daily collections, clapping their hands loudly to demand payment in exchange for their blessing. According to common belief, a blessing from a transgender woman is quite auspicious, whereas a "curse" is dangerous. So, they often make shop owners prime targets for collection, since businessmen are keen to avoid bad karma, lest it cost them profit. In Tuticorin, where most residents know each other, people readily relinquish coins or small notes to avoid attracting the evil eye. Bypass Road, a busy highway used by trucks transporting salt, rice and other goods from Tuticorin harbour, is the district's primary hub for transgender sex workers. Many of their clients are ostensibly heterosexual truckers and rickshaw drivers. The women wait by the side of the highway and then lead their clients into a nearby field with tall grass. The going rate for oral or anal sex is 200 rupees. Thanks to Rangeela, the women carry condoms and are tested for sexually transmitted diseases every three months. Interestingly, the women are also taught to use some tricks whenever required or possible. Since sex work is conducted mainly at night, there is only the moonlight for illumination, and using a combination of lubrication and careful positioning, they can use their clenched thighs or cupped hands to simulate penetration.' Madhu smiled as she recalled Malar, Rangeela's young daughter laughing about this sleight of hand. '"Most of the time we cheat them, because it's safer and easier and the men don't know the difference!" was what that cheeky young thing told me, Shino!'

Malar, who called Rangeela 'Ma' but still lived with her birth family at the time, had undergone surgery recently. She had become close to Rangeela after abandoning life in a local seminary, where she was training to be a priest. There, as she later reported, she was raped by a senior priest, who threatened to expose her inclinations toward femininity, which he had discovered through private conversations.

It seemed that Malar still regularly attended Sunday mass in Tuticorin and was now concerned about paying for her paruvam adaithal, or puberty, a confirmation ceremony for members of the hijra community that takes place forty days after the penis is removed. Trans women, not only from the district but throughout the state, witness and celebrate friends completing their transition into womanhood.

As all of us sat in silence after our long conversation, we heard a loud noise followed by the piercing wail of the nadaswaram—the classic double reed wind musical instrument from south India that was the herald of both temple processions and funerals. The crowd surged as one, rushing towards the sound. But what was happening? The mystery pulled us forward, our feet moving faster than our thoughts.

NARTAKA NAIYAGIGAL: THE DANCING DIVAS

We made our way through the sea of people. It was around 10 a.m.

As we approached the source of the noise, the crowd peeled back to reveal two elegant nartakas, or transgender performers, locked in a fight—not of their fists but of their pride. One of them—a vision in a well-draped yellow sari—loudly demanded of the other, 'Why don't you learn the lyrics before you sing?'

'Ommala okka!' a tall woman with jasmine in her hair, swore vehemently. 'Don't talk nonsense—this is my third consecutive year singing here.'

'Po di! Go away! You don't talk nonsense. Performing here often does not mean you're a good singer.'

As their argument got more intense, they began swearing more and more violently, drawing the attention of everyone around them. A middle-aged man came forward and said, 'Please sing for us. We've come here to see you dance and sing and not fight.'

'Tambi kekuthu la! Sing for the brother!' cried the other transgender women who had been mute spectators until then.

The woman in the yellow sari drew herself to her full height and sniffed angrily. 'If you want me to sing, she will have to go. If that is all right with you all, I will proceed.'

Everyone nodded, and a hush fell over the crowd as they waited for her to begin. A beam of sunlight broke through the skies and fell onto the ground as if creating a natural spotlight for her. Stepping into it, she sang with great skill and enthusiasm while the others danced to their heart's content.

'This is kummi attam,' whispered Madhu beside me.

Deeply woven into the fabric of Tamil cultural traditions, kummi attam is an ancient village dance usually performed without musical instruments. In this art form, women make a circle clap their hands in a rhythm while singing and dancing together. One of the women leads the singing while the rest follow.

In some of the southern states of India, kolattam (originating in Andhra Pradesh and Tamil Nadu) and dandia (originating in Gujarat) also take on a regional form. Usually performed during Navaratri celebrations, kummi, also linked with garba, is performed around a lit lamp or a figurine of a deity placed in the centre. Sometimes, the dancers lock hands to form a circle, moving as one. These dances provide the opportunity for large groups to come together and participate in the celebrations.

Through the centuries, on festive occasions, performances have been based on stories of Krishna. More recently, they have been performed by men, women or by both in pairs.

As the performance continued and the crowd watched spellbound, a troop of photographers arrived, their shutters firing at the speed of light as they captured each nuance of the moment.

Once the kummi attam was over, most people around the temple complex seemed to disperse. Many transgender women returned to Viluppuram, while the locals returned home. A few visitors lingered to rest in the temple premises for a while. Manu and I bid farewell to Madhu and Chinna Ponnu and walked away from the crowd towards the relative peace of the paddy fields. We soon found shelter under a sprawling tree, and within what seemed like seconds, we gave in to the temptation of a nap.

We woke up a short while later, refreshed and ready to dive back into the festivities. The sun had shifted in the sky: it was early afternoon. On our way back, we noticed a couple of trans women in their night clothes walking towards us through the deserted paddy fields. The narrow path forced us to cross each other, and as they came closer. I asked if I could photograph them. We learned their names later, but the one who smiled first was Anandhi and her equally pleasant companion was a dusky beauty called Kalai. They were both from Vellore.

While we were introducing ourselves to them, there was a sudden movement and a young girl peeked from behind Kalai's shoulder. We had missed her completely! She turned out to be their thirteen-year-old daughter, who seemed quite shy.

'That's our daughter—she's in school, and we are trying to give her a proper education,' said Anandhi.

'Which standard are you in now?' I asked.

'Eighth, anna,' said the little girl with her eyes fixed on the ground.

'*Inga irukarathillaye iva than chinna thirunangai.* She is the youngest among the trans women here,' said the proud Anandhi.

Anandhi's gentle words made the girl feel even more shy.

We were told later that the little girl had been abandoned by her 'biological' family because of her sexuality, but Anandhi and Kalai had given her a home and family. One of the most magical operations of the universe is the way people who have faced rejection and abandonment find each other and form a community that offers a sense of belonging. After talking to us for some time and allowing us to take some photos, the little girl became more comfortable around us. As I listened to the story of their small family, I was impressed by the fact that Kalai and Anandhi, despite not having stable jobs due to societal discrimination, were not only managed making ends meet but also supporting their daughter's dreams in the best possible way—by making sure she felt proud of who she was.

It was through my conversation with Kalai and Anandhi that I

saw how adoption stitches the disjointed and abandoned members of the transgender community together. A single trans woman typically adopts four to five children, providing for their emotional and financial needs and teaching them to be independent. But most of all, by opening her heart to these children and giving

them ample love and care, even on the behalf of their 'biological' parents she secures their survival.

As I walked back to the temple, I thought: *Perhaps this is how change takes place—one happy, beloved, safe child at a time.*

REALITY CHECK

After the sun had receded a bit, late in the afternoon, the crowds seemed to be more than ready for the next round of events. As I observed the crowds, I saw that there were different groups of transgender women milling about, and each group had their own purpose for visiting the festival, especially in the aftermath of the sacred thali ceremony. The largest and most common ones are the groups that are constantly followed by men teasing and flirting with them. These men gather around the thirunangai, asking for selfies and hugs—occasionally even making inappropriate gestures and seeking attention in ways that border on physical harassment.

Interestingly, the men who come to Koovagam generally dress well while presenting themselves to the trans women. What they seem to seek is quite simple: the comfort of falling asleep in each other's arms, the thrill of a new and perhaps fleeting romance.

Another group is referred to as the 'chameleons', individuals who can change their appearance and roles with great ease. You might see them waiting alone in the fields, not revealing their face or identity. Sometimes the same person will change many outfits. They often seek out young men and in secluded areas, they offer companionship and intimacy.

There are other trans women as well, those who have undergone gender-affirmation procedures. For them, this place and this event mark a very important milestone—they are a moment of validation, a proud celebration of their femininity. The joy they experience when people accept their true identity is priceless.

Then there is the group of shopaholics who spend their evenings browsing in the bangle stores, exploring the circus area and indulging at the food stalls. This festival is where the denied pleasures of the whole year are finally given free rein.

Finally, there are the elders of the community, those silver-haired trailblazers for whom Koovagam is both a homecoming and a pilgrimage. Dressed in saris, wearing their joy and dignity proudly, they come to relive memories, share laughter and honour companionship that has only deepened with time. In Koovagam, they can be themselves, free from judgement and prejudice.

The evening began to deepen around us and the changing light seemed to transform the setting we had been in all day. I felt a strong wave of emotion as I watched the people around me, so profoundly immersed in the now. I kept thinking about how, for the trans women who come to Koovagam, this festival is all about self-love. The freedom, confidence, attraction and respect they receive here are the dreams their community has chased since time immemorial, against all odds. Witnessing it all unfold brought me a deep, wholesome joy.

While I was a film student, my world was much smaller. I had very little life experience, and my perspective was mostly urban. I hated stepping out of my comfort zone and would refuse to meet

new people. Having grown up in a city, I had not experienced the various aspects of rural India and its complex beauty.

What brought me out of the confines of what I knew was a piece of brutally honest advice that Amal Thamby, a friend and a staff member at the film institute gave me. At that point, it had hurt me but it also radically changed me. He had said, 'You know *nothing*. Think outside your narrow view of life and you'll see the wonders of the world. If you want to learn, you have to break out of your comfort zone. Don't be a whiner and get yourself out there!' Through my journey to Koovagam, I had done just that. The crush of bodies, the intermingling smells of fried food and malli poo, the laughing transgender women's faces—all this was my real education.

'Manu, I'm so happy to be here—to be alive and witness this,' I said, my voice almost getting lost in the noise around us.

'I agree. It's beautiful—and so special,' he replied quietly.

As the night progressed, the festive mood set in and the crowd swelled. From an isolated village to the centre of thrumming activity, Koovagam had transitioned into the Amsterdam of Tamil Nadu.

WHEN THE EVENING GROWS LATE

As nightfall approached, a familiar fear resurfaced: Where would we spend our second night around Koovagam?

Over the course of my life, I've realized that magic often comes disguised as luck: a miracle, serendipity or mere coincidence. Later that evening, our great carrier of fortune drove past us in a white Ambassador. The car came to a stop and Madhu, her daughter and Chinna Ponnu stepped out. We joined them for a short walk through the temple grounds.

'Shino, Manu, don't even think about staying elsewhere. Come to the guest house again tonight.'

Our faces lit up instantly. Lady Luck was truly on our side during this trip.

The events planned for the night began to gain momentum. In unspoken solidarity, both Manu and I put our cameras away for a while, choosing instead to witness the spectacle with our eyes rather than through a lens.

A few minutes later, we made our way to the circus grounds. It was around 8.30 p.m.

The large colourful tent in the middle of the ground was irresistibly inviting and the audio system repeated the same announcement on loop: '*INNUM SILA SEETTUKAL MATTUM THAN*! ONLY A FEW TICKETS AVAILABLE!' The excitement outside the tent only heightened our curiosity to see the show ourselves. With the crowd swelling around us and tickets selling out fast, we rushed to grab ours before it was too late. Nothing could have prepared us for what we were about to witness inside the tent.

THE ANIMAL INSTINCT

The circus tent was quite large, capable of seating more than 300 people at each show. Soon, the show began in a flash of glittering lights and loud Tamil film songs. There was a solo performance followed by a group dance. The dancers were tall and beautiful, wearing colour-coordinated clothes with similar patterns, but there was absolutely no synchronization between any of them. The performance was an unmitigated disaster!

The crowd, nevertheless, continued applauding and demanded that the dancers show more skin. The dancers seemed a little emaciated, but they became energized when the spectators threw garlands of money on stage. I was amazed by how easily the men in the audience lost their composure—the mere glimpse of curves, a sway of the hips and they were completely uncontrollable.

Soon, another set of dancers dressed in risqué outfits got up on the stage and started performing. Both Manu and I were restless—we realized that we could not sit around for another ridiculous performance and decided to leave. When we reached the entrance of the tent, we noticed there was a long queue waiting to get in. The security guards refused to open the gate and let us out. Just then, two dancers approached the gate carrying bottles of fresh juice. When they asked to be let out, one of the guards said, 'We're afraid that these people might run inside if the gates are opened.'

'And we're afraid that we'll starve to death if you don't open the gate. We've been performing for hours, we must eat something, let us go outside,' said the taller dancer with a smile.

The guards relented. But as soon as the gates were opened, the situation turned ugly and violent. Many people rushed towards the dancers, phones in hand, clamouring to get a picture with them.

'Akka, these bastards are touching us without our permission. All we wanted to do was eat after dancing for hours,' she cried.

One of the trans women, stout, muscular and visibly furious, asked her who had misbehaved with them. The dancers pointed out a few men in the crowd. With tremendous energy, the older woman jumped at one of the men and kicked him hard while shouting, 'We know the full depth of human depravity and nothing can shock us anymore, do you hear?'

The dancers kept sobbing, shaken and humiliated, while their sisters gathered around them to comfort them. Some of the men immediately fled the scene, while others stayed rooted to the spot, witnesses to both violence and resilience.

Clammy hands reached out to grab the dancers and grope their bodies. We tried our best to push some of the men away but we were powerless against their growing numbers. To protect themselves, the dancers sat down on the ground, desperately shielding their bodies with their bare hands. We watched helplessly as the crowd continued to violate them. Suddenly, with a huge burst of strength, the taller danced broke free and ran towards a group of older trans women standing outside the gate.

A WALK WITH MY CONSCIENCE

Once we had walked a certain distance from the tent, we bought a few watermelon slices and a cup of mixed fruits. It must have been around 10 p.m. Just as we were about to leave, I overheard a conversation between two men nearby.

'These aravanis who make money by dancing in the circus should not have been treated so poorly.'

'Forget it, it doesn't concern us,' replied his friend.

'What do you mean? You can't just brush it off! Incidents like what we have seen tonight, these brutal violations, they will keep happening if we don't change things. Those men had no remorse, only arrogance.'

'This happens every day, da. These dancers have no choice but to deal with it. Anyway, we need to worry about something else, there are no vehicles out of Koovagam this late. Let's go.'

And with that, the duo left.

The ignorance of their words echoed in my mind, but I was also alert to another logistical problem: we had to reach the guest house in time, too.

We requested an auto driver to drop us off at Chengalrayan Mills. Even though the auto had no room for additional passengers, he did not deny our request. The roads were jammed, however, blocked on both sides by vehicles. About ten minutes later, we became restless. We jumped out of the auto and realized that we had to find our way back on foot that night.

We must have walked for over an hour. Around midnight, we

reached the guest house. The security guard handed us the room keys and my mother's dupatta. Happiness filled my heart as we entered the room. Strangely, the reason behind this feeling was not that we could finally rest after a long day, but that I had learnt to accept things that were not in my control. Manu went to the bathroom to freshen up, while, I lay down on the bed, covered in dirt as I was, and dozed off immediately.

A MAGICAL NIGHT

2 MAY

It was 4 a.m., and from inside the room, I saw a bolt of lightning flash across the sky and light it up. As I watched through the window, the wind and the rains intensified. I noticed that some of the branches had been torn off the trees outside.

The storm was the fiercest I had ever seen—the clouds seemed to burst and the falling rain sounded like gunshots in the night. Thunder rolled across the sky, seemingly cracking the world into two and revealing the fury of the gods. It felt like the end of time, but it was in that moment that I felt truly alive. A loud clamour of thunder pierced my eardrums. I got up from my bed and closed the window.

Suddenly, I remembered what Rajendran anna had said the previous night. 'Our Koothandavar will bless this land with rain on a full moon night.'

THE CALM AFTER THE STORM

The next morning, the earthy smell of moist soil dragged us out of our beds. Tiny droplets of water clung to the leaves, and the wet trees and plants seemed to have a new life in them.

I couldn't help but think: *With the marriage of the aravanis completed, last night would have been their first one together. The rains and heavy thunder felt like god's applause for the cosmic union that had taken place last night.*

As we stared at the sodden landscape, Manu, his voice still thick with sleep, shared what he had read about the festival last night, after I had dozed off. Much of the lore we knew already then, from the multiple conversations with the locals and our own endless research on the internet. But each time, some new nuances leapt at us, as Manu's account also showed. Kuttantavar or Koothandavar or Aravan or Iravan, the son of Arjuna and Uloopi, the Naga princess, is worshipped in south India by Tamils and the followers of the cult of Draupadi. We knew this and that the festival is celebrated with much pomp in Koovagam, and the legend of Koothandavar can be found in the Kuttantavar Sthala Purana. The story of Aravan is also found in the earliest surviving Tamil version of Mahabharata, the Paratavenpa by Peruntevanar, composed in the ninth century.

What Manu told me next cleared the mystery around the origin myths of the festival better than ever before. Ahead of the Mahabharata war, a narabali, or human sacrifice, was required for the Pandavas to emerge victorious. The person to be sacrificed had to possess all thirty-two lakshanams or moral qualities. Only three people fit this criterion—Krishna, Arjuna and Aravan. The former two could not be sacrificed, hence it was decided that Aravan would be sacrificed for the greater good. Aravan agreed but on the condition that Krishna would grant him three boons.

Manu narrated the legend with a certain gravity as he read his notes from his phone. 'The first boon was that Aravan should come back to life and die a glorious death on the battlefield. As per this boon, Aravan comes back to life and is killed by the demon Alambusha during the war. The second boon, as per the cult of Draupadi, was that Krishna should allow Aravan's severed head to witness the entire war. The head is mounted on a pole that is erected in the battlefield. This boon has parallels in the Telugu legend of Barbarika. In Rajasthan, Himachal Pradesh and Garhwal, it appears in the story of Khatushyam ji. For his third boon, Aravan said he did not want to die a virgin as he wanted the glorious death of a self-fulfilled warrior. To ensure this, Krishna transforms himself into Mohini and marries Aravan, and they spend the night together. The next day, Aravan is sacrificed to goddess Kali who blesses the Pandavas with: victory in battle.'

'A few of these strains we already know, Manu.'

'Yes, but there's more. This is where the other story we heard comes into play. Aravan's alleged revival before he is martyred again. After the war, when the Pandavas are discussing their victory, Bhima is quite proud of his contribution to the war. But when he is asked who turned the tide for the Pandavas in the war, Aravan responds that it was Krishna's chakra and Draupadi, who drank the blood of the warriors in her avatar as a goddess, that won the war. This angers Bhima but before he can hurt Aravan, Krishna drops Aravan's head into a river full of reeds. Aravan is then reborn as a child and is adopted by the king of a distant land, who finds the infant, while he is on a hunt. The child grows up and kills the demon Kuttacuran, who, it is foretold, can be slain only by a child born of reeds. This boy goes on to be called Kuttantavar (the one who killed Kuttacuran) During the festival, Aravan's story and his sacrifice are performed as a therukuttu, or street theatre. His legend symbolizes not only sacrifice and devotion but also rebirth and continuity, owing to his ability to witness the war even after his death. Some scholars believe

Aravan's sacrifice is a reworking of the serpent sacrifice theme in Tamil epics ...'

After nearly five minutes of this monologue, Manu paused to take a breath. As he looked around the rainswept garden, he spoke again. 'I also read about the temple and its associated beliefs last night and it is said that there are different versions of the story from different temples and places. One such is the Draupadi cult,' said Manu.

'So, what rituals does the Draupadi cult follow?'

'Devotees of Draupadi commemorate the Mahabharata war by conducting an annual festival known as Patukalam. This festival usually begins with a koothu, or drama, to reenact Draupadi's wedding. During the festival, the actor playing Draupadi (and other women participating in the public ceremonies) laments the death of Aravan and the other heroes of the war. There is some variation in the length of the Patukalam festival and for the day allocated to performing the koothu of Aravan's sacrifice, or kalappali, but wherever the ritual kalappali is performed, that place is declared to be the battlefield of Kurukshetra.'

It was clear that Manu was utterly captivated by this story for he took out his notebook and laptop and began referring to a new set of notes now. 'In Irunkal in Tamil Nadu, this koothu is usually performed sixteen days before Patukalam day, the last day of an eighteen-day festival. In Singapore, however, the koothu is performed on the day of the new moon in the Tamil month of Purattaci, which is usually in September or October of the Gregorian calendar. In shorter ten to twelve-day festivals, the koothu and ritual of Aravan's kalappali are performed on the concluding night of the festival in paces like Bangalore and in and around Chennai—at Sowcarpet, Alandur and Poonamallee.'

He paused to check his notes and then continued: 'However, there are also some variations in how Aravan is represented in the festivities. While permanent wooden Aravan heads are used in temples in Chennai and Puducherry, Aravan's head and body are made of clay in rural areas, and both are destroyed at the end of the festival. At Tindivanam, a headless clay and bamboo body of Aravan is modelled, showing him in a heroic position, kneeling on his left knee and holding a bow. A clay head is then ceremoniously fixed, making the effigy about 7 feet tall. The officiating priest first takes a sword, striking pieces from the head. Then, a pumpkin is sliced into thirty-two pieces, symbolizing the thirty-two pieces of Aravan's sacrificed body. Next, the deity is fed his own "blood", represented by the blood of a goat, sacrificed to him in advance. His body from the neck downwards is then covered with a bloodstained white cloth. Finally, blood-soaked rice is sprinkled on Aravan's face. Followers of the Kuttantavar or Koothandavar cult believe eating this rice, recovered after the ceremony, can induce pregnancy.'

Manu had hit a jackpot last night, clearly. He went on about the other related festivals as well, sensing my intrigue.

'Now listen to this. In Chathiram Karuppur near Kumbhakonam, a 25-foot statue of Aravan is constructed horizontally and placed on the ground. His story is then re-enacted, and one of the actors, believed to be possessed by Kali, kills a rooster over the statue's neck, symbolizing the sacrifice. Again, blood-soaked rice is distributed to devotees, especially childless women. Similar rituals associated with a symbolic sacrifice and blood-soaked rice are performed in Melacheri, Alandur, Poonamallee and Viluppuram. A goat is sacrificed in Alandur and Poonamallee, and a rooster is sacrificed in Cuddalore, Patirikkuppam and Viluppuram. In the Cuddalore, Thanjavur and Viluppuram districts, Aravan's head is hoisted to an elevated position to watch over the Patukalam and the symbolic re-enactment of the Mahabharata war.'

'My god, so many varying perspectives and myths. Where did you find all this?' I asked Manu.

'After all the information we got yesterday, I was quite curious to understand other perspectives of this history. So, I updated my search prompts and found countless other resources we had not yet seen.'

I was flummoxed yet deeply moved to realize the histories behind this event that we were witnessing in our own time.

We left the guest house after our conversation and while we were on our way to the temple, crossing the fields once again, we noticed that the violent winds during the night had whipped the trees and crops out of shape rather mercilessly. Yet, in contrast, the kids in the village seemed charged up and free-spirited. A group of young girls was redirecting surplus water into the fields. Koovagam and its people seemed to have transformed overnight.

THE LESSONS OF THE INFINITE

2 MAY

It was here at last. After a stormy night, the eighteenth and final day of the festival had arrived. At the Koothandavar temple, Lord Aravan's enormous head was placed on a chariot, paraded through the village and later cremated. Traditionally, the aravanis continue to mourn the death of Aravan for weeks after the event is over. As we made our way through the village, we saw a few trans women resting in the shade of the trees, the remains of the previous night—including bottles of liquor, empty food packets and condoms—strewn all around them.

At first, the aravanis we came across would not permit us to take pictures. But soon, a family of them welcomed us into their circle. I sat with them, quietly observing how each one helped the other to get dressed, adjusting sari pleats, sharing accessories and fixing each other's make-up with care.

When one of them finished draping her sari and looked at herself in the mirror, I thought, *How beautiful she is and what a lovely smile she has!* After taking a few pictures of her, I said, 'Great make-up, akka,'

The woman got very excited and asked, 'How do I look, tambi?'

'Like a princess,' I said at once.

She blushed prettily and said, '*Inakiku mattum thaan unaku nan rani. Nalaiku thirumbi kuda pakka matta nee*. I am a queen just for this day. Tomorrow, I will go back to being neglected.'

QUEEN FOR A DAY

While I was making more images, Manu reminded me that the ceremony where the thalis are untied was going to start soon and that it was about a kilometre away. We prepared to make a move.

The path we took seemed like a living marketplace. Jackfruit sellers had set up stalls there and were carving open the giant specimens for their countless customers. An old man on a bicycle was selling buttermilk. A few women were selling topped with chilli powder. Small children darted past us, running towards the ice cream stalls excitedly.

EN ROUTE TO THE MAIN EVENT

A procession comprising those who had been ceremonially married the previous day, trans women, men and children, now walked solemnly towards the next event, the most dramatic one of the festival—the untying and breaking of the thalis and the beginning of a long period of mourning. Many were accompanied by their birth or found families. The crowd was overwhelming. By the time we arrived in the main compound, from where the procession was supposed to commence, a part of the ritual had already begun, and it soon became quite clear that the previously vivid energy of the place had metamorphosed into something macabre.

Watching the aravanis prepare for the widowhood rituals, I felt an intense sadness. Their paths in life had led them through so much suffering and pain. Perhaps the series of rituals that were to follow offered a purging of these intense, accumulated emotions. Presently, the pujari raised his hands brusquely and then mercilessly broke the bangles worn by some of the aravanis closest to him, ripped off their thalis and threw these into the fire. What followed was raw, unfiltered grief. A horde of spectators and photographers surrounded the now-widowed trans women, who wailed in despair, beating their chests, taking the flowers out of their hair and wiping off their make-up. They smeared the kumkumam across their foreheads like fresh wounds, the vermilion streaks marking where devotion for their divine husband once lived. They cried loudly in groups, hugging each other and expressing their sorrow in the form of an oppari, a traditional Tamil funeral song. While they did indeed grieve the death of Aravan, their voices also seemed to rise in a lament for the pain of every loss, every rejection, every oppression they had ever endured.

The wails of the mourners, aravanis as well as the others, swelled into a crescendo of despair. They began crying so loudly, it seemed

as if they hoped to summon the gods themselves to Earth to witness their pain. The air thickened as their cries echoed around the temple grounds, and the place spiralled into chaos. In that moment, I could see their souls and their physical selves as two separate entities, as if the soul had broken free of the limitations of the flesh.

I felt extremely helpless, a mute spectator in this sea of mourning aravanis. I could feel the heart-rending howls crawl under my skin. In some ways, I was also confronted with an existential crisis in that moment. What could I as an artist and photographer do to help those who suffer in this world? *The responsibility of an artist is to bear witness*, I thought. I have always believed that if our inner world becomes alien to us, one of the ways to ground it, to find an anchor and a purpose, is to bear witness to the lives of those who surround us and who in turn witness us. It is, in my opinion, the act of witnessing, that makes us real to each other. Real and human.

And so, amidst the tear-streaked faces of this spectacle, I did the only thing that made sense. I picked up my camera and bore witness to the visceral misery of the heaving sobs, my viewfinder framing the tender yet ferocious beauty of unadulterated grief. Every time my shutter snapped, capturing images of these souls moaning, crying and purging their life's sorrows, I accepted that not everything beautiful can be possessed. Nor can it last forever.

I also realized that happiness demands real sacrifice—the kind that strips you bare until nothing remains but your unshakable core.

These women knew this truth in their bones: the ritual of grief was both the beginning and the ending, the fire that clears the field for new growth.

The sound and the fury of the mourning ceremony soon subsided, and a heavy yet peaceful calm descended on Koovagam.

The trans women began to walk.

Manu stopped at a juice stall and asked the vendor, 'Where are they going?'

'The widows will now bathe and change into white sarees. The event happens in a quiet place near the fields.'

'How do we get there?' I asked.

'Follow any one of the aravanis without a thali. But don't get too close.'

'Why, anna?'

'Not all of them are welcoming and you could get into trouble,' warned the man.

We thanked him for the advice and began following the crowd slowly.

Although we had been walking for a while, even though we were making progress, the site of the ceremony appeared to be some distance away. We stopped under a banyan tree, drank some water and rested briefly, allowing the crowds to make headway.

'So, what next?' asked Manu.

'I think I want to understand Aravan's sacrifice and how it ties into Tamil traditions. I need to explore how his sacrifice lives on through the actions of the aravanis at the festival and how they pay homage to it, because I don't think it's simply a myth for them—it seems like a clan memory,' I said.

Manu nodded silently and closed his eyes, as if he were meditating.

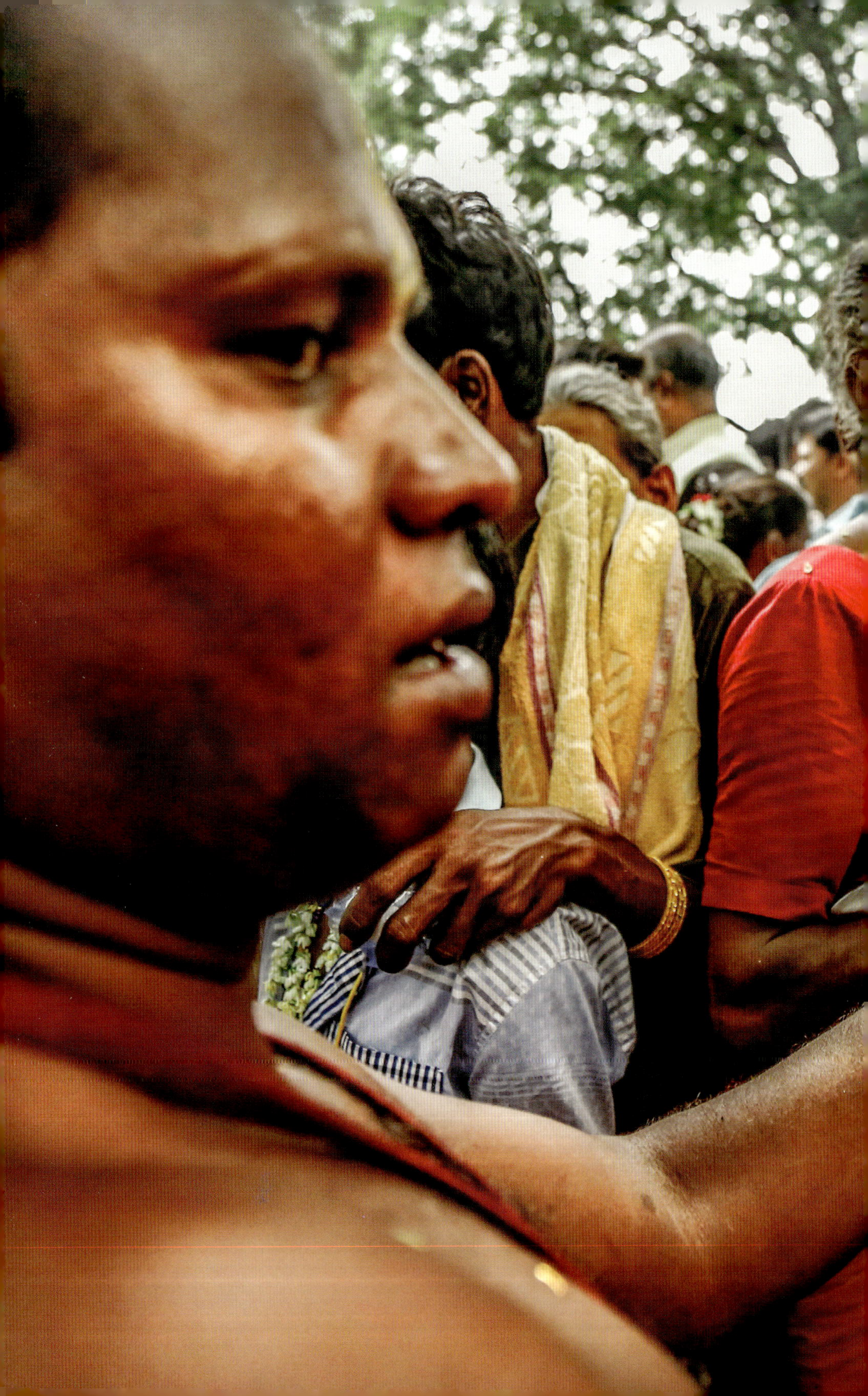

CUTTING THE THALI LOOSE

Soon enough, Manu dozed off, and I looked around the field idly for the next few minutes. Then I picked up my phone and started researching Aravan's sacrifice. At first, the same articles and stories I had already read online kept showing up in the search results. I decided to dig deeper into the digital archives and eventually landed on some arcane bits of information.

Aravan's pre-battle sacrifice was the prime element in the Tamil traditions. After Krishna granted his boons, Aravan was ready for the sacrifice and went to the battlefield. While Yudhishthira was worshipping Kali in his hall of weapons, Aravan took off his epaulettes and chest plate. He then cut his body into thirty-two pieces, one piece for each of his thirty-two bodily perfections or lakshanas. These pieces were then offered to Kali by Yudhishthira.

After being stripped of his flesh, Aravan was only left with his head and skeleton. Krishna advised him to pray to the Naga, Adi-Shesha, his maternal grandfather. Adi-Shesha coiled himself around Aravan, became his flesh and restored his body—which is when Aravan returned to the battlefield before he was martyred again. To fulfil the boons, Krishna orchestrated his heroic death by making one of the enemy's warriors strong enough to defeat the mighty Aravan. Krishna selected Alambusha. Then, depending on the version of the story one believes in, Krishna either advised Alambusha to assume the form of Garuda, or he sent the true Garuda to assist Alambusha. At the sight of Garuda—his perennial 'eagle' adversary—Adi-Shesha uncoiled in fear, leaving Aravan unprotected. Seeking the opportunity, Alambusha beheaded the weakened Aravan. In a villu pattu performance, this event is depicted by covering the actor playing Aravan with a white cloth from the neck down. Legend also holds that Aravan's spirit may possess the actor at this point. Sometimes, a chicken is sacrificed on stage to signify the martyrdom. In some cultures, an elephant is sacrificed to the goddess, paying homage to Aravan's own sacrifice.

In both the Koothandavar and Draupadi cults, Aravan is believed to have been granted a second boon which allowed him to witness the entire eighteen-day war with his own eyes: his severed head is mounted on a pole with a panoramic view of the battlefield. Indeed, evidence of this boon is found in a fourteenth-century version of the Mahabharata.

As I had read earlier, one of the three boons granted to Aravan enables him to be married to a woman before he is sacrificed, also entitling him to the right of cremation and funerary offerings (bachelors were traditionally buried). This strain is usually found almost exclusively in folk traditions. No woman wanted to marry Aravan, however, fearing the inevitable doom of widowhood. In the version prevalent in the Koothandavar cult, Krishna solves this dilemma by taking on his female form, Mohini the enchantress, marrying Aravan, and spending his wedding night with him.

The most widely accepted version of the myth in Koovagam also speaks of Mohini's mourning as a widow the next day, after which Krishna returns to his masculine form for the duration of the war. In villu pattu performances, a stylized wedding ceremony is followed by Mohini's abrupt departure, taken to signify that the marriage is unconsummated. Another version, popular within trans communities, suggests that Aravan's wish was for 'coital bliss' and explicitly frames the marriage as consummated.

This third boon, related to marriage, is not, however, uniform across all folk traditions. In other legends, Krishna arranges different pre-war marriages. In Thanjavur, the marriage of Aravan and Mohini is unknown; instead, it depicts Aravan as married to Paravanacciyal, the daughter of Krishna's cousin Satyaki.

Some others theorize that the myth of the first boon—heroic death—and third boon—marriage—originated with the Koothandavar cult, while the myth of the second boon—

witnessing the battle—originated from the Draupadi cult. The Koothandavar cult, hence, ritualizes both the heroic death and the marriage ceremony, which is enacted by aravanis. In the Draupadi cult, however, it is the clay head of Aravan, fixed to a post and witnessing the re-enactment of the war, that is prominently ritualized.

Additionally, texts of the Draupadi cult from Thanjavur focus only on this second boon, omitting the other two. The pre-battle sacrifice is incompatible with the first and second boons; but the cults have their own explanations. The self-sacrifice before the war conflicts with dying a heroic death during the war, and both are incompatible with living to see the full duration of the war. The Koothandavar cult resolves the first dilemma, by maintaining that Aravan's body regenerated itself after the sacrifice and that Aravan went on to die a heroic death later in the war.

The Koothandavar cult is not overly concerned about the second boon that allowed Aravan to observe the war. Conversely, the Draupadi cult is not overly concerned about the first boon that grants him a heroic death; they resolve the second dilemma by claiming that Aravan was able to watch the entire war through the eyes of his severed head. A third view harmonizes all the boons, proposing that Aravan's body reconstituted after the sacrifice; he then fought heroically until being decapitated on the eighth day, and then observed the remainder of the war through the eyes of his severed head.

I had been reading frantically about all these cults for a while when Manu shook me out of my reverie. Just then, another group of trans women walking towards the site passed by, and without much thought, we fell in step with them. I noticed that Manu was looking down at his feet, walking as if in a trance, his gaze fixed on the dust clinging to his shoes.

I wanted to know what was going through his mind, so I said, 'Imagine, Manu, if every sari here turned white.'

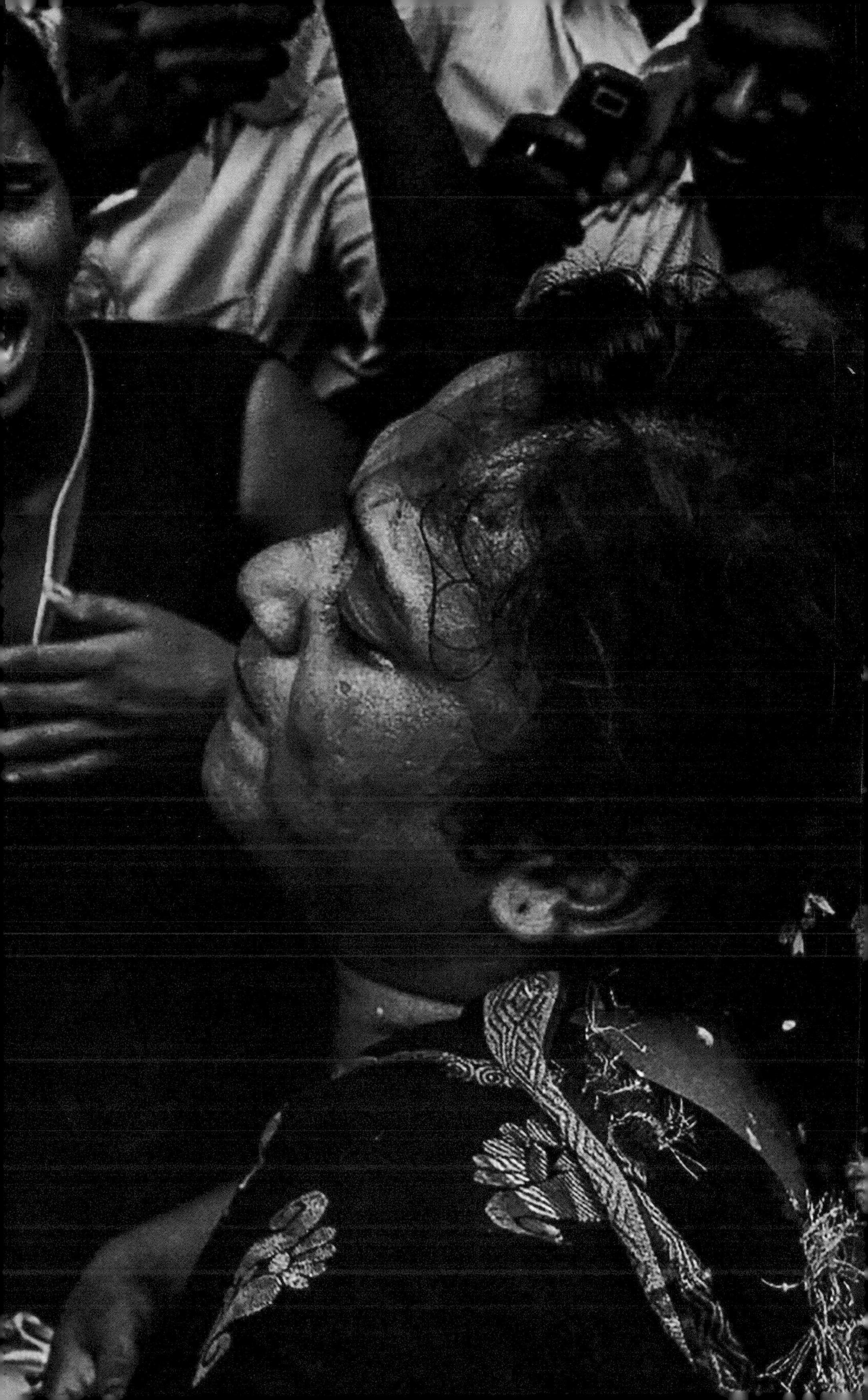

He did not hesitate as he responded, 'Then this field would only host ghosts walking in daylight.'

I understood at once what he meant—Koovagam would be devoid of colour, of defiance, of strength.

The afternoon sun hung high in the sky; the air puffy and gloomy. A few hours ago, the grounds were packed with devotees in riotous colours, but now they were all dressed as spectral figures in white; the transformation both beautiful and terrifying. We saw some trans women bathing in groups near a small pond, scrubbing dirt and the previous day's make-up off their bodies. Others stood still as their companions draped their white saris on them. The festival's vitality had dissipated like mist under the morning sun, leaving behind these pale figures moving through fields of melancholia. These were the widows of Aravan.

As we watched, the solemn moment of mourning was turned into a spectacle: multiple media people moved through the crowds, their microphones and cameras at the ready, about to package the women's grief for mass consumption. It was clear that this festival was only an assignment for them. These photographers made the mourning trans women walk performatively for videos, pose for pictures and finally, they tried to tell them what to say as well. As one trans woman from Bangalore started talking about the historical importance of the event and the challenges that the community continues to face, the journalist interrupted her and said, 'We'll add all that later as additional text. Right now, just give us the lines we asked you to.'

Most people tend to see the world as black or white, deliberately blinding themselves to the many shades that make up life. Their perceptions are shaped by social media, television and films; all of which can be ambiguous at best, or misleading at worst. These platforms can either glorify or vilify a community as per their whims, and popular media consistently reduces trans people to malicious stereotypes.

Most of the trans women were grieving silently now. We moved deeper into the clusters of women gathered in the fields. They moved in quiet solidarity, their eyes focused on the ground, hands caressing each other in quiet comfort.

'I wish people could look beyond these foolish and simply *wrong* views of these women and speak of and to them as equals, Manu. But most people remain ignorant. The aravanis call out to god for help in their moments of strife, but even the gods don't seem to come to their rescue.'

Manu looked at me and after a brief pause, he said, 'Perhaps there isn't a god.'

I could not bring myself to click photos of the aravanis. Something seemed to whisper to me: *This is not what you came here for.*

I walked away, making my way into the fields, letting the quiet swallow me whole. As I was walking towards a tree, I noticed a trans woman changing clothes behind it. When she saw me approaching, she covered her breasts with her clothes gracefully and looked at me with her piercing eyes. She didn't seem afraid as much as measured and curious about the interruption.

As I slowly reached for my camera, she stood there like a dove, still and alert, her bright eyes still locked with mine.

'Do you mind if I take a photo of you?' I asked. 'You'll look even more beautiful if you smile.' There was something original and raw about her beauty.

She turned her face towards the camera, and a smile surfaced—half hidden, serene and strong—on her lips. That's the moment I released the shutter. Her white clothes represented the soul in its purest form, with no hatred, nor ego. Her eyes glittered with a mix of unshed tears and anticipation. There was the subtlest hint of joy on her face, an acceptance of what life had to offer. Her hands, pressed against her chest, spoke not of modesty but of the power of the femininity she held inside her. The wiped-out sindoor on her forehead indicated a life she had left behind. Some strands of her thick hair framed her arresting face; and the red cloth tied around a low-hanging bun added a stunning contrast to the setting. Her attire wasn't only about the ability or will to dress up as a woman—it also signified her transition from one life to another.

After I had clicked this photo, I walked back from the fields to where I had left Manu, the powerful moment and subject still lingering in mind. Something inside me had shifted in that encounter. It had stripped away whatever little distance remained between me and the events I was witnessing in Koovagam.

I found Manu taking photos where I had left him and we decided to go back to the temple. On our way, we saw a lone trans woman walking towards us. She was tall, lean and beautiful.

I wanted to ask her a few questions, but as she drew nearer, I hesitated. The juice seller's warning about some transgender individuals being offended at being approached rang in my ears, but I decided to take the chance.

'Hello, akka. We have come from Chennai for this festival, and I was wondering if you could spare a few minutes to speak with us? We would like to ask a few questions.'

She paused, looking at us for a moment, then smiled and nodded gently.

'What is your name, akka?' I asked.

'I'm Aishwarya, it means prosperity or wealth,' she replied.

'A beautiful name. I wanted to ask you, being here amongst the crowd . . . how do you feel about yourself? Or your inner self and your community?' I asked vaguely, unsure of how to phrase the question. My words fumbled out, half-formed, but it seemed as though my good intentions were clear.

'Emotions? About being a transgender?' she asked, her voice flat—

like someone who had been asked that too many times before.

I nodded, words still evading me.

'You see, I studied hotel management in Chennai,' she said. 'I worked at a five-star hotel and earned 50,000 rupees a month. But within a few months, people began to talk about my body language, the tone of my voice, the way I carried myself ... They were able to sense that I had a feminine side. My co-workers supported me, but I was troubled by the comments from my seniors during team discussions, non-regional co-workers who formed a group to tease me about my daily activities, the security guards who smiled suggestively while opening the gate, the shop owners who gave me cash and asked me to leave their shops when I went to buy things. Every day was a struggle. And then, one fine day, I burst out. I couldn't take it anymore, and I refused to be invisible.'

'What happened then?' I asked.

'I decided that I wasn't meant to be in a place where people didn't accept me. So, I moved on.'

'Did you discuss this with your family or relatives?'

'It's been five years now,' she said softly. 'I still remember the day my family found out that I wasn't a "regular" man, as they wanted me to be. They begged me to leave. To them, I was an embarrassment. A stain on their reputation. So, I left home. The challenge in the real world is that if you don't have a proper education, you cannot find any honourable work. That's the main reason my sisters take up the sex trade. Do you know how it feels to be sexually assaulted and criminalized on the streets? How easy it is for that to happen? I've seen many transgenders be rejected by their families and resort to begging for food for their survival or fall into the pit of prostitution.'

'How did you find the courage to leave your family and live on your own?' I asked.

'My desire to become a woman, to be who I have always been, made me strong,' she said without a moment's hesitation.

'Do you ever go back to your family?'

'I have suffered so much to become what I am today. Why should I bother about the birth family that rejected me?' She paused, glanced around at the other trans women walking, laughing, resting nearby. 'These people—they are my family now.'

'In that case, I have one more question, akka. In Hindu mythology, there are many transgender gods, right?'

'Yes, there are,' she said as she patiently waited for me to make my point.

'Most of us pray to these gods and seek their blessings, but why is it that people's attitudes change when they see a transgender in real life?'

'We don't want them to treat us like gods—just like human beings. This world is clay and air, and man is neither a vegetable nor an animal. He is a thinking being, who, in fact, has been placed here to rise above the animal form, to aspire for higher purposes, guided by higher motives and divine intention. The challenge is to find the right idea and the right path to harmony. The real struggle isn't survival, tambi. It's convincing the world that peace begins when you stop seeing differences as threats.'

Her words settled into the deepest part of my soul. I was speechless. I wanted to ask Aishwarya what brought her back to Koovagam every year, but the answer was evident. This was her festival. This was her place, where she was accepted for who she was. Just then, Aishwarya disappeared into the crowd to shed her colourful sari and change into the white one she was carrying.

When I think back to that moment now, and think about what Aishwarya said to me, I am compelled to consider the urgent need to remould ourselves progressively and work towards the highest

Amma

levels of both individual freedom and social unity. Social change begins at the family level, in our respective homes. We need to break free from harmful stereotypes and teach our children that trans people have a right to exist in this world with dignity and respect, that they have the same aspirations and dreams as we do. Workplaces need to be more transgender-inclusive with initiatives like equal-opportunity hiring, infrastructural support such as restrooms for the third gender, mechanisms for strong action against misconduct and harassment, better, more equitable access to medical insurance and healthcare policies for gender minorities. Most important, we need to be more inclusive and welcome trans people in our society by treating them as equals and standing with them in their fight against discrimination. Legal recognition of their rights can go a long way to accelerate these changes.

A major milestone in the fight for transgender rights came in 2014 with the landmark judgement of Supreme Court—in the *National Legal Services Authority (NALSA) versus Union of India [Writ Petition (Civil) No. 400 of 2012]*—delivered on 15 April, which recognized transgender individuals as a 'third gender', affirmed their right to self-identify their gender and directed the government to grant legal recognition to ensure equality and non-discrimination. The court also classified them as socially and economically backward, making them eligible for reservation under the Other Backward Classes quota. In July 2016, the Supreme Court had to reprimand the central government for failing to implement its own directive, particularly in terms of job and education reservation. Activists also strongly criticized the 2016 draft bill for the Protection of Rights of Transgender Persons, arguing that it diluted the spirit and intent of the 2014 ruling. The bill was eventually passed on 10 January 2020, promising legal recognition, prohibiting discrimination and mandating the welfare of transgender individuals. As per the 2011 census, there were 4.87 lakhs persons in India who opted for 'other' in gender category. This figure is assumed as the population of non-binary persons in the country. The Transgender Persons

(Protection of Rights) Act, 2019 and its Rules, 2020 is a big step towards ensuring the safety of these citizens. The government also constituted a National Council for Transgender Persons under this Act through a notification dated 21 August 2020. These are all essential steps, but there is still much to be done.

Aishwarya's simple but powerful words also stirred some childhood memories I'd tried to forget. When I was a kid, one of my neighbours was applying mehendi on her daughter's palms. I asked her if I could also get something on my palm, but she only laughed and said boys mehendi wasn't for boys. A few years later, when I heard that my best friend had passed away, I burst into uncontrollable tears. Another friend came up to me and casually said that men shouldn't cry. Prejudices are maintained by these normative micro codes and guidelines in our lives.

It's said the perfect man should have a thick beard and broad shoulders. But why? What if he has a soft face, a gentle presence and doesn't fit the so-called 'manly' mould? I'll tell you what will happen: people will assume he's weak. They'll treat him as inferior. What if I start to wear a bindi from tomorrow? Will my parents, friends, society and culture accept this? Will they treat me as they have treated me all my life? Is there a fixed definition of how a man or a woman should look, feel, or behave like? Sadly, yes. Society has already drawn those lines for us. And we, consciously or unconsciously, become the living examples of those expectations. I realize more strongly every day that we need to do better and allow for differences to co-exist peacefully, rather than treating them as threats to the norm, as Aishwarya told us that day.

A NEW BEGINNING

2 MAY

By late evening, the crowd at Koovagam had almost completely vanished, the vendors were calculating their incomes for the day and some 'widows' were rushing through the fields, carrying jackfruit and other items they had bought. Some public transport vehicles were parked in one of the paddy fields. In the midst of all this, I felt how the experience in Koovagam, the pilgrimage that it had become, had seared memories into my soul. In Koovagam, I had seen up and close a living tapestry that represented courage and love.

There was Madhu, the bold lady we met at the event had who graciously offered us a safe place to stay in during the nights. Chinna Ponnu, who made sure that we ate properly through it all. Rajendran anna, who generously shared with us the history of the village and the festival. The always smiling Subash anna and his family who had welcomed us with kaalan every time we got lost in the crowd. The determined Anandhi akka and Kalai akka, who wanted to give the world to their daughter. Aishwarya akka, who had found the courage to quit her job because it conflicted with her identity.

What would have happened if we hadn't met these humans who gave us love in such abundance? They never once asked us where we were from or what caste we belonged to or how educated we were. Nor did they judge us by our appearance. They shared their lives with us and showed us that the world is big place, and we can all co-exist peacefully if we can learn to look beyond our narrow prejudices. I often think about what the old man at the tea shop had said to us, 'Have a little faith. There's magic in the night, and if you only believe, you'll find magic everywhere.' And so there has been.

Just as we were beginning to leave the festival compound, I noticed a figure, someone who had been noticed by very few people. She wasn't fashionable, didn't utter a word and seemed to deliberately hide herself to escape public scrutiny. I looked around for Manu, but he was nowhere to be seen. I went to sit silently by this lonely woman's side for a while. I saw the white sari she was wearing—a symbol of purity. Her eyes never looked up at the shenanigans all around us. It felt like she had known and walked away into a deeply isolated place internally, away from years of pain and memory.

Minutes later, dark clouds gathered over Koovagam. She picked and folded the clothes she'd left out to dry and packed her things. Before leaving, she looked at me, her eyes focused on mine and caressed my cheek gently. I felt a strange numbness for a while after she had left.

I felt as if I was being born into a new life, and that all the ideas and habits of the past could no longer be of any use to me. What once seemed like an achievement had only been preparation for this bigger event. I felt as if I had done nothing until that moment, as if I had not lived, as if I was only entering the lane that leads to life in earnest after Koovagam.

Later, Manu and I found each other again. We wandered through the thinning crowds, letting the last of the festival wash over us. It had begun to rain and we stood beneath a wide canopy of trees, with some others.

Manu noticed that I was quiet and asked why I looked so gloomy. I couldn't answer him. My heart felt hollow yet, too full of things I did not understand. He asked again, and then again—gently, persistently. But I remained silent.

The breeze shook water from the trees and for a moment it rained under the branches where we stood. Soon it started to drizzle and

then just as suddenly, it stopped. I wanted to tell Manu how I was feeling as honestly as I could. I wanted to explain the heaviness in my heart, the strange shift inside me, the feeling of having touched something so much larger than myself. But I just couldn't find the words. There are times when silence is a poem.

What am I to you?
What am I to myself?
What am I to anyone?
I ask the questions of everyone.
I am one in all.
I am all in one.
I am infinitely in love.

Off I go,
To the lands that show,
Magic in halves,
Magic in the whole.

An unfinished poem,
That I am,
Looking to be complete,
By the folklore of the discreet.

For this place,
Let me unbecome
The person that I think I am,
And let me become
The person I actually am.

And so I ask again,
What am I to you?
What am I to myself?
What am I to anyone?

I am the very soul of someone.

MEET THE PEOPLE

Subash anna and family

Ram Manu Prasad—my fellow traveller (left) and Madhu with her daughter (right)

Anandhi and Kalai with their family

Aishwarya akka (left) and a group of trans women helping each other at the event (right)

ACKNOWLEDGEMENTS

To my pillars of support, Mr P.V. Cherian and Mrs Anila Cherian: thank you for giving me the freedom to explore my own and unique direction in life, Pappa and Ammu.

I would also like to thank:

Shalini Somanath, for showing me the right path to pursue and pushing me to take the initial steps.

Prashanth Ramadoss, my brother and best friend.

Sharath Ettan for keeping my spirits up throughout this journey.

Huge love for Sandeep Shyam for retouching and optimizing the images.

And finally, but immensely, M. Aarthi, Reina Maria, Snehalatha Menon, Teena, Nagalekshmi S.V., Shakthi Srinidhi, Kavaraj Balasubramanian, Shankar Nair, Varun Venkata Krishnan, Gowthaman Natarajan, Vignesh Chellapan, Murali Dharan, Anand G.K. and Praveen Leo for being real and genuine throughout the years it took me to write this book. Thank you for this infinite love.

My work is dedicated to the memory of Aashique Ignatious, my best friend who stood by me through thick and thin and believed in me enough to make this journey possible. We miss you, Aashi. Come back to us soon …

ABOUT THE AUTHOR

Shino Cherian is a travel photographer and aspiring filmmaker. After obtaining his Engineering degree from SRM University, Chennai, he studied Cinematography at Neo Film School, Kochi.

Cherian spent the first few years of his career working in the film industry and advertising firms in Chennai. He filmed a documentary in the Western Ghats, *Patterns of Life: Prana*, which won critical acclaim and was released on Mubi India and Amazon Prime in 2020.

His arduous journey to the Koovagam festival, which celebrates the transgender community, paved the way for his debut photobook, *Souls of Someone.*

HarperCollins *Publishers* India

At HarperCollins India, we believe in telling the best stories and finding the widest readership for our books in every format possible. We started publishing in 1992; a great deal has changed since then, but what has remained constant is the passion with which our authors write their books, the love with which readers receive them, and the sheer joy and excitement that we as publishers feel in being a part of the publishing process.

Over the years, we've had the pleasure of publishing some of the finest writing from the subcontinent and around the world, including several award-winning titles and some of the biggest bestsellers in India's publishing history. But nothing has meant more to us than the fact that millions of people have read the books we published, and that somewhere, a book of ours might have made a difference.

As we look to the future, we go back to that one word—a word which has been a driving force for us all these years.

Read.